Primary Teacher Training

Ajoy Chatterjee

CRESCENT
PUBLISHING CORPORATION

[*The responsibility for the facts stated, conclusions reached and plagiarism, if any, in this book is entirely that of the Author. And the Publisher bears no responsibility for them, whatsoever.*]

Primary Teacher Training

First Published : **2014**

ISBN 81-8342-057-5

Published by :

CRESCENT PUBLISHING CORPORATION
4831/24, Prahlad Street,
Ansari Road, Darya Ganj,
New Delhi - 110002
Ph. : 23272541, 23257835
Fax : 91- 011- 23257835
e-mail : campusbooks@hotmail.com

Typesetting by :

Arjun Computers
Delhi - 110051

Printed at :
Roshan Offset Printers
Delhi

Preface

Primary school teachers develop schemes of work and lesson plans in line with national curriculum objectives. They challenge and inspire pupils to help them deepen their knowledge and understanding. They facilitate learning by establishing a relationship with pupils and by their organisation of learning resources and the classroom learning environment. They develop and foster the appropriate skills and social abilities to enable the optimum development of children, according to age, ability and aptitude. They assess and record progress and prepare pupils for the standard assessment tasks. They link pupils' knowledge to earlier learning and develop ways to encourage it further.

Primary teacher training has to suit the needs and demands of present days' world. In many countries newly qualified teachers have to serve an induction or probationary period, normally of one year. During the induction period, teachers are monitored and supported, have a reduced timetable, a designated mentor and work on areas identified for development during their initial teacher training. In-service training is available to all teachers, both in house on training days and in training centres run by education authorities. This training covers a wide range of topics, such as curriculum issues, special needs, subject leadership, pastoral care, new initiatives and technology. Some teachers pursue higher qualifications on a part-time basis, such as masters degrees in education or business administration, depending on their career aims. Professional qualifications for school managers are also available. Modern teacher training scheme enhances the career of especially talented teachers, offering early responsibility and higher salaries.

This book comprehensively describes the problems and methods of primary teacher training. It is divided into ten chapters. It is hoped that this book will prove useful to the teaching departments and institutions, teachers of educational administrations as well.

Ajoy Chatterjee

Contents

1 Introduction

The overall quality in education mainly depends on the quality of teachers and a sound programme of professional preparation of teachers is essential for imparting quality education. Teaching is an art which can be inculcated through a series of well designed activities in respect of education and training of teachers and is equally valid for professional preparation of teacher educators. The teacher educators would not only be training pre-service and in-service trainees but would also be associating themselves with several other activities.

New strategies and techniques of material development, the changing approach to evaluation, intensive interactions with the community, creating an activity-based environment in the training institutions, acquiring skills for resource mobilisation and several other such competencies at mastery level would be essential for professionals to function as teacher educators. Changes in the school curricula would be faster in the near future.

Teacher educators will be expected to display a deeper understanding of the issues pertaining to access, participation and attainment in their specific regions or areas. They need adequate professional competence to conduct such surveys and studies would reveal the region specific and area specific issues and problems which would help the functionaries of the education department and the community. They will prepare the trainees in responding to these issues during the training period and also in schools subsequently. The professional quality of teacher educator will determine the quality of the training of teachers, both pre-service as well as in-service. The professional level at which teachers are prepared would, in turn, determine the quality of school education.

Teacher educators have to be fully familiar with the school realities, social environment and community expectations to realistically perform the challenging tasks before them. On the professional side, teacher educators need to be actively associated with policy formulations, implementation strategies and monitoring of programmes. At present, the only programme which is often treated as preparing teacher educators is that of M.Ed. Scrutiny of the curriculum of most of the M.Ed. programmes would reveal that these have not been specifically designed to prepare teacher educators. There are some M.Ed. programmes where provisions do not exist for writing a dissertation.

In India, the University Grants Commission (UGC) has been organising national and regional level workshops for improvement of the teacher education programmes. Through various schemes it offers financial support for seminars, workshops and research projects for teacher educators for such themes as higher education, educational technology, non-formal education, population education, environmental education, research methodology, etc. The National Institute of Educational Planning and Administration (NIEPA) organises programmes for Principals of Colleges of Education, Heads of University Departments of Education and other administrators concerned with teacher education. The SCERTs and State

Boards of Teacher Education organise continuing education programmes for teacher educators on teaching methodologies for new subject areas and on innovations in education.

Some University Departments of Education organise seminars, workshops, and orientation programmes for teacher educators on teaching, development of instructional skills, interaction analysis, teaching behaviour, educational technology, guidance and counselling and research methodology. Certain Colleges of Education and University Departments of Education have been upgraded as Colleges of Teacher Education (CTEs) and Institutions of Advanced Study in Education (IASEs) for taking up innovations in teacher education. NCTE after its establishment in 1995 as a statutory body, has initiated several programmes aimed at enhancing professional competence of teacher educators. These include seminars and workshops in the area of human rights and national values, indigenous thoughts in education, indigenous approach to teacher preparation, institutional networking and capacity enhancement and production of good quality enrichment materials for teacher educators. These institutions have considerable experiences in organising training and development activities. Based upon the experience gained they will have to evolve programmes of sequential nature with in-built mechanism for assessment and impact evaluation.

In the absence of an appropriate policy of recruitment, specially at the pre-primary, primary and elementary stages of teacher preparation, the manpower in the institutions of teacher education does not necessarily possess the professionally required qualifications for the preliminary stages. At the pre-primary stage one comes across teacher educators who have passed high school or higher secondary examination and possess a certificate in teacher training, not necessarily meant for the pre-primary stage; graduates or those with higher qualification with absolutely no training background or with the background not appropriate for that stage or level. As regards the primary and elementary stages, the teacher educators, generally, possess graduate or higher qualification with teacher training mostly at the B.Ed. level. There are serious lacunae in the recruitment policies in as much as the professional qualifications prescribed are not stage-specific and mostly not suited to the education of teachers for the stage or level concerned. This situation calls for fresh thinking regarding recruitment policies for teacher educators and well-planned programmes of education for teacher educators.

Education and training of teacher educators has to focus its attention on the new role of teacher educators on the problems which reflect the emerging global trends in education and the overall needs and aspirations of the people in India. It has also to deal with specific problems confronting teacher education institutions and to make teacher education more responsible and responsive. It also has to encourage teacher educators' continuing professional growth. In addition, there are certain practical problems as well. For instance , what would be the basic qualifications of teacher educators at various stages of teacher preparation? What would be the requirements in respect of the core education courses and for the organisation of procedures and practices in the institutions. Answers to several of such issues have to be sought in the very rationale of providing professional education. The rationale behind the education and professional training of teacher educators lies in providing qualitative instruction through well-designed programmes of professional education.

The following objectives can be comprehensively identified for the programmes of preparation of teacher educators :

- to develop competencies and skills needed for preparation of teachers and teacher educators
- to enable them to organise competency-based and commitment oriented professional programmes
- to enable them to develop pedagogy relevant to the education of teacher educators
- to acquire an understanding of the needs and problems of teacher educators and teacher education institutions
- to develop skills related to management of teacher education institutions
- to develop competencies of curriculum development and preparation of learning and evaluation materials
- to enable teacher educators to acquire capabilities to organise in-service continuing education programmes
- to enable them to organise need-based and commitment oriented on the job training
- to develop competencies for evaluating educational programmes and teaching learning materials
- to develop the capacity of examination, analysis, interpretation, elaboration and communication of educational ideas
- to relate education and the national needs and develop critical awareness about Indian realities
- to enable them to understand the relationship between Indian ethos, modern technology and education

- to promote the global perspective of educational development with special reference to the developing countries.
- to enable them to undertake meaningful educational research.
- to develop the capacities to reinterpret Indian heritage, culture and values to meet the requirements of the present-day Indian society.
- to develop the capabilities for self-directed and life-long learning.
- to enable them to appreciate and adopt emerging communication technology and innovative practices in Indian context.

Pre-service Education of Teacher Educators

The present system of pre-service education of teacher educators is characterised by lack of perspective in terms both of contents as well as qualifications. For instance, while it is well accepted that the B.Ed. qualification entitles a person to teach at secondary stage , it is doubtful if the M.Ed. programme adequately prepares a person to become teacher of secondary school teachers.

The existing M.Ed. programme has little provision of training in and working out teaching and evaluation strategies suited to the needs of teacher trainees. And yet one finds M.Ed. degree holders entrusted with the responsibility of teacher preparation not only at secondary stage but also at the pre-primary, primary and elementary stages of teacher preparation. Likewise, while the B.Ed. qualification legitimately entitles a person to teach at the secondary stage, it cannot, at the same time, be accepted as a good enough qualification for being a teacher educator at the primary stage. The existing B.Ed. programme is designed mainly to teach high school students and not for preparing primary school teacher educators. Thus, it is imperative that the professional qualification of teacher educators is made stage-specific suited to the needs of teacher trainees of different categories. It is time for seriously considering designing of definite programmes to prepare teacher educators rather than depend on the conventional B.Ed. or/and M.Ed. course.

Education of teacher educators has necessarily to correspond to teacher preparation programmes. It is nonetheless necessary to consider alternatives and institute programmes like M.Ed. (Teacher Education) catering to the needs of stage-specific and category-specific preparation of teacher educators alongside general M.Ed. programmes. Existing M.Ed. courses in Indian Universities are by and large academic in nature and not adequately professional in content. In as much as the Master's level courses in Education need to be formulated for making it a professional course, some additional areas of study will have to be introduced with changed orientation.

Programme Development

An altogether fresh look is necessary for first developing need-based programmes for the preparation of teacher educators and then working out well planned strategies for implementing these programmes. Needless to say that the preparation of teacher educators would concern itself with the relevant theoretical courses as well as the consonant practicum. At the theoretical level, the choice of pedagogical inputs has to be guided by various contexts and their educational and professional concerns. In addition to theory courses, specialisation courses with reference to teacher education have to be included. The theoretical courses will have a bearing on the practice of teacher education. It will be necessary to develop competencies and skills in prospective teacher educators relating to their work situations. What goes on in teacher training institutions by way of educational programmes and activities has to be reflected in the education and training of teacher educators. It essentially implies that the preparation of teacher educators has to be made an integral part of the system of teacher education.

It will be pertinent to evolve a pedagogy relevant to the stage or category specific programmes. It will lay due emphasis on societal goals, values specially those enshrined in the Indian Constitution, higher order learning processes, curriculum development and theory and practice of educational research including action research. Competence to carry out research and innovations needs to be acquired by all. Training in curriculum development and preparation of learning materials is inalienable aspcct of entire process of teacher education. Similarly, development of evaluation materials would result into more effective utilisation of evaluation in teacher education institutions.

The practical work has among other things necessarily to include internship programme by way of attachment to the stage-specific and category-specific teacher education institutions. This will give the prospective teacher educators an adequate knowledge of the total functioning of teacher education institution, the improvements needed and also provide insights into the problems and issues concerning maintenance of institutional plant, classroom management, organisational climate of the institution etc. As for practice teaching, the main thrust has to be on a variety of techniques such as team teaching, micro-teaching, panel discussion, seminar, demonstration, etc. as integral part of classroom-teaching-learning-evaluation procedures. Practical work other than internship and practice teaching has to develop competencies and skills in organising activities concerning work education and working with community as per the practical work requirements in the teacher education institutions.

Continuing Education of Teacher Educators

The present provision for continuing education of teacher educators is inadequate in respect of both quality and content. Planning in respect of in-service education of teacher educators needs to be evolved for different stages and levels. The major thrusts in respect of programmes for teacher educators among others, may be as follows:

- Designing short-term programmes for those who are already placed in these institutions.
- Specific short-term induction programmes for those who do not have the experience for the stage they are supposed to be working at.
- Identification of certain university departments of education and Institutions of Advanced Study in Education as institutions which may work mainly for teacher educators. They may focus on induction training, recurrent training, orientation programmes, research studies and surveys, curriculum development, preparation of training materials, evaluation strategies and techniques, use of educational technology, media and others.
- Establishment of institutions for preparation of teacher educators for special education at different stages.

These may be open to primary and secondary trained graduates willing to become teacher educators. Such programmes need to be designed with particular focus on the practicum that would familiarize the trainees with school situations in totality.

– Networking of various institutions and organisations for designing and carrying out collaborative programmes by pooling and sharing of resources.

With the policy focus changing to quality and relevance of education, it is necessary that only those, who are professionally competent, committed and willing, are charged with the responsibility of preparing teachers for the nation. Teachers for various stages, levels and categories are prepared professionally by teacher educators. The quality and character of teachers therefore, would largely depend on the professional education of teacher educators. Towards this, it is necessary, therefore, that their education should be given a new orientation and improved qualitatively and adjusted properly with the demands of the new curriculum.

2

In-service and Pre-service Teacher Training

Teacher education has an essential and inalienable component of practical work including student teaching, internship, field work, working with the community, work education, etc. The country needs teachers with different orientation and specialisations to manage educational programmes. The curriculum for teacher preparation, in future has to emcompass the broader canvas which is consistently emerging before the teachers and shall continue to change at a much faster pace in times ahead.

Teachers shall have to take a global view of the new trends, strategies and practices, and focus on indigenous heritage and thoughts which could fit in the local and national situations. Transplantation of alien educational ideas and practices has not been found rewarding in developing countries. The teacher education programmes shall focus on competencies and commitment in much greater magnitude in future. Such a transformation in teacher preparation strategies would emerge only after due familiarity and adequate appreciation of indigenous thoughts developed over decades. Gradually an indigenous approach and strategy would emanate and replace the alien practices that have remained in vogue in teacher education over the decades.

TEACHER EDUCATION SPECIFIC TO EARLYCHILDHOOD

The objectives of teacher education specific to early childhood include the following:

- to prepare teachers for facilitating physical, mental, moral, social, aesthetic and linguistic development of children
- to acquaint them with the knowledge of child psychology
- to cultivate social sensitivity, affection for children and respect for their uniqueness
- to acquaint them with techniques of caring for children and enable them to identify their needs
- to provide experiences and organise activities that promote children's self-concept, creativity and inventiveness
- to enable them to select, prepare and use different kinds of resource materials
- to develop a sense of involvement with and appreciation of local resources and their utilisation
- to develop an acquaintance with basics of Scientific and Technological Literacy
- to develop a repertoire of children's games, songs and literature
- to empower student-teachers towards creating learning readiness among young learners.

In the preparation of teachers for this stage, the main thrust will be on sensitising prospective teachers about change and its implications - cultural, social, economic, etc. as also with the change in the learner through motivation and learning.

Future need will be to empower the teacher to observe change, interpret it and adopt, adapt, modify, consolidate, accelarate or reject the same. It is, however, expected that the course on Emerging Indian Society' will enable the intending teachers to know about the rights of child, human rights, legal literacy, community dynamics, knowledge of national and local festivals, emerging trends in community life and social living, prominent personalities in various walks of life, familiarity with factors and forces affecting environmental and population equilibirium, knowledge and appreciation of places of historical and cultural significance and landmarks and trends of development.

Another theoretical input which is intended to be given to the prospective teachers is regarding knowledge of nature and scope, status, problems and issues concerning early childhood education in India. These need to be understood in terms of Indian reality and perspective, foundations of child behaviour etc. In addition, it may include, among others, progress of early childhood education, its historical development, problems, need for looking at it from the point of view of diversity, flexibility, local relevance and specificities, and the agencies involved in the process of promoting early childhood education. Basic to designing programmes and activities for children at this stage is a thorough understanding of various aspects of growth and development of the child which the prospective teachers will be required to internalise.

Since, it is being recommended for intending teachers of pre-schoolers, it will be necessary to know about the fundamentals of early childhood care and education. Most of the training programmes of teachers for this stage will have major concentration on organisation and activities as mentioned above. In addition, the teachers will be required to have a practical training at early childhood education centres and the like. At this stage, greater emphasis will be given on propagation of early childhood care.

Teacher is expected to recognise commonalities and specificities in order to shape the personality of children for living together in a perpetually changing complex society. The suggested theoretical components included in the framework are essentially, meant for broadening the intellectual horizons of intending teachers who will become conversant with the culture and traditions of the country with due appreciation of the diversities.

The seeds of democratic living are sown from the beginning of childhood and education needs to be regarded as a vehicle for maintaining equilibirium in the growth of individuals from childhood to adulthood. It would be worth experimenting with modular approach of teaching combined with interventions of realistic nature by way of field trips, visit to museums, zoo, educational excursions, visit to mountains, forests, intermediary interventions with real life situations and through audio-video devices, wherever possible.

Teaching in teacher training institutions be directed towards empowering prospective teachers to enable to use their experiences in actual work places for enhancing growth and development of young children. There is to be a planned amalgam of theory and practice in a way that these two constitute a continuum of experiences. The teaching of theoretical components, in addition to what has been elaborated above, will combine various methods and approaches like lecturing, tutorials, seminars, term-papers, discussion groups, gaming, role planning, etc.

The teachers at this stage are being initiated into and introduced to the art of teaching. Teaching to them is romance with innovativeness and inventiveness. It is love for children. It is caring for children. It is seeking for optimum enrichment of experiences of children. It is providing happiness to children. It is making their stay joyful in schools. The early childhood education includes transacting developmentally appropriate curriculum which includes within its fold concept development, convergent and divergent thinking, creative activities, language acquisition, etc.

It is an arduous task of equipping prospective teachers with competencies and skills needed for making the learning experiences of a child joyful and memorable. It must be admitted that the training of pre-school teachers is complex and full of challenges. The pedagogical aspects of training will be planned around activities and programmes for children, attending to their needs, identifying interests of learners by gender and their background, identifying children with special needs and devising strategies for their optimum growth and development, organising games, recreational activities, plays, etc.

Theory and practicum have to be linked and integrated in the training process. Much of what goes by way of practicals is intrinsically related with pedagogy and much of the essence of pedagogy lies in the practical work. The practical work may include comprehensive case studies of children including children with special needs, gifted children, children coming from different socio-economic and cultural backgrounds, etc.

Development and use of schedules, assessment checklists and other evaluation tools and techniques will form an important aspect of practicum. The maximum utilisation of environmental and community resources can be done only when the teacher is thoroughly conversant with environmental resources. Community survey, therefore, is one of the several activities of practical work which requires systematic exploration. The practical work of the prospective teachers will centre around evolving and devising programmes and activities for physical, psychomotor, cognitive, emotional and other aspects of development. Health and hygiene, habit formation, are certain other areas which require practical work. In addition, art, drawing and painting, using clay/plasticin, music, dance, recreation, story telling, games, and physical activity are a variety of examples of other practical experiences which a student teacher will be required to undertake for creative expression of children.

Evaluation for the theoretical component may include assessment of sessional work, term-papers, participation in seminars, discussion groups, etc. besides semester examinations which can be oral, written, practical and objective type. The written tests have to be reliable, valid and representative of the totality of experiences. Different tools and techniques of evaluation can be used for assessing the pupils' growth. Visits to and partcipation in activities of Anganwadis, Balwadis, Day Care Centres will make a part of training towards understanding the dynamics of working with children and educating them. The evaluation of this component is will be in the form of a cumulative record of the performance of the intending teachers. External evaluation of practical activities will defeat the purpose as the practical work is, by and large, activity-based. It is essentially sessional work, day-to-day internal assessment, feed back and monitoring.

Universal Elementary Education

The constitutional provision of providing free and compulsory education to all children upto 14 years of age includes both the lower primary and upper primary classes, that is from class I to class VIII. There seems to be a compelling need for having multiple models for preparing teachers - for primary and upper primary classes. Incidentally, in a number of Elementary Teacher Education Institutions (ETEIs) in the country, the nomenclature of the training programme from pre-service training of primary school teachers has been changed to pre-service training of elementary school teachers. But in actuality, the transformation in programmes has yet to take place effectively. There are three distinct possibilities of designing courses in teacher education for elementary stage:

a) Teacher education programme exclusively for primary school stage (Classes I to V).

b) Teacher education programme for elementary school stage (Classes I to VIII).

c) Teacher education programme exclusively for upper primary school stage (Classes VI to VIII).

In view of the requirements of Universal Primary Education and Universal Elementary Education, only the first two alternatives are being recommended. However, the third suggested above, could be attempted by offering credit oriented modular courses after successful completion of primary teacher education programmes. It is significant to note that we have nearly 5.98 lakh primary schools which are mostly in rural areas as compared to upper primary schools numbering about 1.76 lakhs only. The formulation of the curriculum framework for the elementary stage will also be guided by general and specific objectives of teacher education and characteristics of curriculum development. The specific objectives relevant to the stage may include the following :

- to develop understanding of the psychological and sociological principles relevant to elementary stage of education.
- to enable teachers to select, prepare and use appropriate resources for organising learning experiences.
- to acquaint them with methods and materials of teaching children with special needs
- to develop among them the capacity to solve the social and emotional problems of children.
- to enable them acquire necessary skills so as to develop curiosity, imagination and self-confidence among children.
- to develop communication skills
- to enable them to mobilise and utilise community resources as educational inputs.
- to enable them to organise supplementry educational activities
- to undertake action research projects
- to enable them to establish mutually supportive linkages with the community
- to enable them to organise games, sports, physical activities and other co-curricular activities.

Curriculum Transaction

The prospective teachers are to be prepared as to enable them to perform successfully in the pre-instructional, instructional and post-instructional phases of teaching. For this, several well-designed approaches like lecture discussion cooperative study, self-study and project methods etc. may be adopted. Depending on the nature of the subject, the teachers may combine different strategies and instructional aids, utilise media supported teaching, organise field trips and practicals and demonstration techniques. In this process due attention be given to children with special needs. The curriculum transaction will have to be adjusted with the needs of students and locally available resources. During the process of teaching and learning, the existing transactional strategies marginally promote the capacity for independent study, self-discovery and self-study and rarely seek prospective teachers' participation and remain one way traffic with the result that the subject matter communicated is partially assimilated and not fully utilised. Teacher education has to inculcate professional commitment, develop competencies and make teacher reflective to deal with specific situations.

Practice teaching, the weakest link of teacher education, possesses the potentiality of converting itself into a strong component if properly organised. The process of curriculum transaction needs improvement and enrichment. Pedagogical analysis of teaching subjects is sure to refine teaching and learning as it will transform the teachers' performance and develop competencies not covered by the method-cum-content approach. With the background of pedagogical analysis and model and demonstration lessons given by the teacher educator, the class room performance is sure to improve if it is supervised in detail by the subject specialist. Work education is an important component of practical work and its potentiality has to be utilised by teacher education for developing certain qualities of character. Community surveys helps to formulate a proper social perspective. The mutually supported school and community interaction helps the teachers to evolve suitable teaching strategies.

The teachers will be required to organise educational activities in school. They have to learn to plan and organise such activities as are essential to provide opportunities for self-expression and lead to development of personality of students. They have to be trained for utilising supplementary materials essential for accelerating and promoting learning among students. The teachers will be required to facilitate physical, social, emotional and aesthetic development of students. Their creative and constructive potentialities have to be fostered. Practical activities suggested in the document will help to achieve these ends. It is, therefore, necessary to organise these activities on continuing basis.

The influence of teachers' personality and behaviour has lasting impact on students. In the selection and adoption of transactional strategies the teacher has to ensure that teaching becomes participatory, cooperative, activity-centred and joyful. The success or failure of the curriculum transaction is ascertained by evaluation done by means of valid and reliable tools. At this stage, evaluation has to be continuous, formative and comprehensive to bring improvement in teaching learning process. Systematic evaluation will enable a teacher to select proper teaching strategies and effect suitable changes in the curriculum process. The evaluation of the pupil teachers at the elementary stage will not differ much from the primary stage and the same principles and similar practices which have been adopted at the primary level may be utilised at this stage.

Formulation of Curriculum Framework

The formulation of curriculum framework for this stage (classes I to V) has been guided by general and specific objectives of teacher education and perceived characteristics of curriculum development. The specific objectives of primary teacher education may include the following:

- to develop understanding of the psychological and sociological foundations relevant to the primary stage.
- to enable teachers to manage appropriate resources for organising learning experiences of children.
- to acquaint them with methods and techniques of caring for children with special needs.
- to enable them to acquire necessary skills so as to develop curiosity, imagination and creativity.
- to develop in them the capacity to understand and analyse the social and emotional problems.
- to develop communication skills
- to enable them to establish mutually supportive linkages with the community focussing on the objective of UPE/UEE.
- to enable them to understand implications of research for teaching-learning and undertake action research and use innovative practices.
- to enable them to organise games, sports, physical activities and other co-curriculur activities.

Transacting Curriculum

Transactional strategies invariably need to emphasise interactive, partcipative and activity-oriented approach. The transaction of curriculum will have place to place and intra- and inter-content variations. The theoretical component of the curriculum can be transacted by lecture-discussion, self-study approach, seminars, media supported teaching wherever possible, tutorials and through practical activities. It is expected that the intending teachers during the course of training acquire mastery of competencies and skills that are basic to making an effective, reflective and committed teacher.

Practice teaching remains to be a weak link of curriculum transaction. This point of view has been substantiated and re-inforced by field surveys conducted by NCTE at different places throughout the country. In this framework, pedagogical analysis of school teaching subjects has been thought of as an essential component of practice teaching. By way of pedagogical analysis a student teacher becomes conversant with the objectives of teaching a unit, the entry behaviour of pupils, classroom management and evaluation strategies. With this background of having looked into the pedagogical aspects of school teaching subjects, the student teacher is likely to become more effective and confident in his/her interventions in the classroom.

As a necessary part of the training of primary school teachers, knowledge of content is given due importance during the course of training. Mastery of subject matter, the insight gained through pedagogical analysis and the foundation courses when thoughtfully integrated and used for classroom instruction will lead to improving the quality of education.

Practical work is an essential component for internalising the theoretical concepts. Thus it will have to be planned on each aspect of theoretical inputs. In addition, practical activities centring around different school experiences, work education, school community interaction, action research projects and other educational activities directed towards development of personality of students will also be undertaken by intending teachers. It needs continuous planning, analysing, monitoring and evaluation throughout the duration of the course which will necessitate the involvement of teacher educators more vigorously than what it is presently.

It is expedient to employ the formative evaluation for obtaining continuous feedback, motivating students and guiding their efforts. There is an increasing felt need to replace external examinations by internal continuous and comprehensive examination system. External system of evaluation, until such times it is replaced, may be perceived as a corrective, moderating and balancing factor. It, therefore, needs to be carefully planned and testing tools made valid and reliable. In different situations evaluation of theoretical component may be based on essay questions, short answer type questions, objective type questions, objective-based questions, oral examinations, participation in discussion groups etc. Evaluation of practice teaching can be done internally, externally or through judicious combination of both. Gradual transition to continuous and comprehensive internal evaluation of practice teaching and assigning grades instead of marks would be a professionally sound step. Evaluation of practical work would also be done internally.

For teaching at secondary stage, the qualification most sought after is one year B.Ed. which is in fact B.Ed. for secondary stage. However, at present, there are several variations for first degree level qualification which are also available. These include B.Ed. (Elementary); B.Ed. (Special Education); which too are programmes of one year duration; B.Ed. through correspondence or distance education mode which is now of two years duration. There are certain other variations in the form of vacation courses or part-time courses which were available before NCTE norms came into force. In addition, there are four-year integrated courses for elementary stage and also for secondary stage. Teacher education programme at this stage, like at all other stages, will include the theory, practice teaching in schools, and practical work in the light of contexts, concerns, profile of teachers and general and specific objectives.

The specific objectives at this stage may include the following:

- to enable the prospective teachers to understand the nature, purpose and philosophy of secondary education.
- to develop among teachers an understanding of the psychology of their pupils.
- to enable them to understand the process of socialisation.
- to equip them acquire competencies relevent to stage specific pedagogy, curriculum development, its transaction and evaluation.
- to enable them to make pedagogical analysis of the subjects they are to teach at the secondary stage.
- to develop skills for guidance and counselling.
- to enable them to foster creative thinking among pupils for reconstruction of knowledge.
- to acquaint them with factors and forces affecting educational system and class room situation.
- to acquaint them with educational needs of special groups of pupils.
- to enable them to utilise community resources as educational inputs.

- to develop communication skills and use the modern information technology.
- to develop aesthetic sensibilities.
- to acquaint them with research in education including action research

A teacher helps in improving the quality of human life in the context of multiple internal and external forces impinging on man and the society. The course on 'Emerging Indian Society', would develop an insight into the nature of indian society, its variety and complexities and making teacher education programme relevant to the community. Ingenuity of teachers lies in first understanding national ethos and then planning for teaching within this framework as a professional.

A professionally trained teacher is expected to identify the strengths and weaknesses of secondary education in India and after having gained insights into the status, problems and issues concerning education at this stage, develop a mental make-up of evaluating the system and utilising the same for promoting excellence in education. A teacher in the classroom has to make adjustments in teaching strategy according to the nature and scope of the curriculum and evaluate the success of teaching in terms of students' growth. The foundations of curriculum, pedagogy, evaluation and remediation need to be laid down firmly during the course of professional preparation of teachers. What kind of pedagogical strategy will give optimum results in specific units of curriculum and in what ways the outcomes need to be evaluated will be the main thrust. Distinct departure from the existing programme is noticeable in including a course on psychology of teaching and learning. The teaching of educational psychology to the B.Ed. trainees was done extensively even earlier but without establishing linkages with actual teaching and learning. The attempt to put teaching and learning together does not in any way undermine the importance of educational psychology. Now the basic thrust will be on teaching - learning processes, group dynamics, learners' background, the internal and external forces of the institution and the community. Psychology of teaching and learning would require adjustments at different levels of schooling and for different grade levels. Foundation courses lend support to refining the education processes implicit in teaching and learning.

Comparative perspective of educational systems in developing and developed countries would enable teachers to acquire a global vision of contemporary context and gain greater insight into ways of improving the quality of education. The understanding of some specific areas of education in detail and in depth is needed for becoming an effective teacher. Guided by this consideration and having been supported through field interactions with different target groups, courses on pre-school education and elementary school education have been included as optionals. Teachers will also be required to get indepth understanding of areas like non-formal alternatives to school education. Similarly avenues for indepth studies in emerging areas of concern like vocational education, environmental education, population education etc. have also been suggested. The message of educational technology has to reach the classrooms in the form of its application. Prospective teacher has to be so equipped in the course of training as to enable him to think of using appropriate educational technology for improving the quality of instruction and for obtaining optimum results in terms of the students' growth.

Physical education has been considered as an integral part of education. In each system of schooling tremendous amount of emphasis is laid upon building up the cognitive base of students and the affective and psychomotor dimensions of human personality, do not receive adequate attention.. A teacher fashioned in the culture of physical education would be conscious of catering to the physical dimension of human personality with concern. The inclusion of this course, however, may not be taken as an alternative to preparing teachers for teaching Physical Education.

The impact of teacher training programmes has not been perceptible over the years in terms of transacting curriculum in schools. Lecture method, mostly taken recourse to by teacher educators, is generally not supplemented by using instructional materials. Interactive teaching, co-operative teaching-learning, self-discovery approaches seldom find place in the day-to-day teaching practices. What is of importance and calls for top priority in the training programme, is to lay appropriately proportioned emphasis on 'why to teach', 'how to teach' and 'what to teach' aspects of teaching. It has to be reflected in the teaching-learning situations planned by teacher educators.

Education as a field of specialised studies is inter-disciplinary in its nature. Since different branches of learning are involved in understanding the presage, process and product variables of education, it is essential that formulation of teacher education programmes adopts a holistic approach in order to promote proper understanding, insight and thinking on matters pertaining to this field. The complimentary character of theory and practice needs to be emphasised at every step.

The prospective teachers are encouraged to organise, express and communicate their ideas clearly in the class. It has to be accepted as a communicative process of an intensive teacher-learner dialogue and renewal of a two-way process as opposed to 'the banking concept' of teaching. The emphasis must be laid on cultivation, formation and development of power of mind in contrast to the prevalent tendency of aiming at the success in examination alone. Student teachers, it is hoped, in classroom transactions, will employ the use of divergent thinking and problem solving strategy. The teacher educators will be required to have clarity of thought in respect of components of a course, objectives of teaching, and their relevance to educational and social goals. One of the approaches may be the modular approach. Each module, though a complete teaching unit, remains a part of the total syllabus with built-in linkages and feedback mechanisms. Learning through this approach can be reinforced by library work, seminar readings, tutorials and small group discussions.

Self-study and self-motivated learning become an integral part of the curriculum transaction. The outcomes would result in better understanding of concepts better leading to mastery learning. The interdisciplinary approach in teaching has to be accepted and implemented for developing comprehensive understanding and vision of educational studies. Learning outcomes have to be assessed continuously, which is the basic tenet of the modular approach. This would help in modifying, adjusting and improving transaction strategies for better acquisition of knowledge. Universities have options to evolve their own examination system. Too much reliance on external examinations, however, would inhibit the progress of moving in the direction of quality education.

There is no denying the fact that practice of education is as important as its theory. Each good theory leads to a good practice and vice-versa. To strike a balance between theory and the practice of education, therefore, is a matter of judicious planning and scheduling in order to give proper direction to teacher education. Changes in the pattern and practices of student teaching have been only peripheral. The content-cum-method approach, wherever attempted, remained limited to the introduction of an additional component of content without fully achieving the objective of integration.

The problem-solving approach, discovery method, competency based teaching learning and the indigenous contributions, like those of Gandhi, Tagore, Aurobindo, Zakir Hussain and several others have the potential for bringing in innovative ideas in teacher education. The application of educational technology, informatics, telematics, cybernetics etc. have yet to make a discernible headway. The learning resources wherever available in the training institutions and the community as also in the schools have not been optimally utilised.

Prerequisite to preparing a prospective teacher can be thought of in terms of providing certain inputs such as, induction programme, an exposure of school experiences with special focus on the educational environment of the school, socio-economic and cultural background of the community constituting the catchment area, observation of classroom teaching and other related activities etc. Induction programme might include acquainting the intending teachers with the school settings, the school programmes - curricular and co-curricular. In addition, they will be prepared for actual classroom teaching and the roles they are expected to assume during the course of practice teaching/internship by way of focussed discussions, demonstration lessons, preparation of lesson plans in a way as to encompass teaching for cognitive, affective and psychomotor development.

Practice teaching is essentially a joint responsibility of teacher training institution and the school involving teacher educators, prospective teachers and school teachers. Teacher educators will help in facilitating and guiding the activities as implied by the pre-instructional, instructional and post-instructional phases through which a student teacher has to progress. The role of a school teacher in this joint effort lies in extending cooperation to the teacher educator and the intending teacher. Various aspects as referred to above will have to be suitably adapted to varying structures and designs at different stages of teacher education.

Practical work other than classroom instruction can be viewed in terms of school and community experiences and activities related to personality and leadership development. Efforts need to be directed towards developing in a teacher trainee certain competencies and skills which would be helpful in the shaping of a teacher for effective role play. It is essentially directed towards capacity building which may embrace, among other competencies, managerial skills , organisational efficiency, leadership skills, democratic attitudes, innovative and creative abilities etc.

The teachers' role, which they will be required to play in the school situation other than classroom teaching, may extend to a variety of activities, such as, maintenance of school records and registers, management of laboratories and library, preparation, repair and selection of instructional aids and equipments, selection and preparation of textual materials, preparation of tests and assignments, admission and selection of students, maintenance of progress reports of students, preparation of school budget and development plans, beautification of school and classroom management etc. The institutional activities within the school environs may include dramatic clubs, stage activities, literary activities, inter-house activities and sports and games, organisation of educational tours, etc.

Interaction between the institution and community is gaining importance in the modern context. One can think of several activities promoting school-community relationship, such as, celebration of birthdays of children, celebration of parents day, activating parent- teacher association for the welfare of the schools, organisation of school and community games, sports and other functions, utilisation of community resources for education, understanding the background of children, celebration of national days in collaboration with the community, environmental education , adult literacy, plantation and social forestry.

Community involvement and school development activities may lead to community awareness generating competency through community - institution interaction activities; mobilising community resources for organising literacy programmes, environmental education, work education programme, health awareness programmes, etc. It is expected that organisation of such activities would lead to developing self confidence and initiative among student teachers and also develop among them positive attitude towards plurality of cultures. The modalities to be employed for organising activities other than teaching for all round capacity building and empowerment of a teacher-trainee will involve joint supervision by the teacher educator and a school teacher. The transaction modes, for example, for motivating adults for making them literate can be through mass participation, folk songs, street plays etc.

The identification of various sports and a variety of activities for cleanliness in the community, collecting success stories and disseminating them in the community, preparing simple write-ups of all the activities undertaken; utilising community resources for the developmental needs of library building, students scholarships, awards, student aid funds, celebration of festivals etc; student-parent-community contact programmes and organisation of welfare shows for better institution- community participation are certain other strategies of transaction of practical work.

A student-teacher undertakes several practical activities which facilitate instruction as also those that relate to management. Relevant to teaching and learning, the intending teacher develops competencies, like identification of support material, skills in preparation of indigenous and low-cost materials, judicious choice and utilisation of material for enhancing the learning and use of community resources for education. The likely activities may include preparation of an inventory of community resources, instructional material, development of software and use of hardware . The teacher-trainee also gets acquainted with the techniques of diagnosis, remediation, guidance and counselling, classroom interaction inclusive of understanding of context variables implicit in the process of teaching and learning, knowledge of educational rules and regulations/laws, in addition to maintenance of cumulative and comprehensive evaluation records, maintenance of school records and is conscious of professional accountability and ethics. It is hoped that most of the activities will be undertaken by the teacher trainee during the internship period of a reasonable duration. Some of these activities will have to be integrated with practice teaching. For meaningful organisation of practical work pre-internship stage may be utilised for demonstration lessons, lectures, simulation, role- playing, micro-teaching etc.

The transactional mode of community related practical work may include interaction between school teacher and intending teacher and members of the community representing parents, panchayats, senior citizens, voluntary organisations, etc. Student -teachers may undertake a case study of a school for identifying its strengths and weaknesses, needs and problems, specific learning problems, such as, drop-outs, drug abuse, behavioural problems, learning difficulties etc. Street plays can be organised by the student teachers to sensitize the community in the ways in which community resources could be utilised and also motivate the community members for greater participation in the school welfare activities. To come to its present form, work education has undertaken a long journey. From Marx's 'combination of productive labour and learning' to Abbot Wood's 'vocationalisation', it came to Gandhi's 'handicraft as the medium of education' and again took the form of Kothari's 'work experience' which Ishwar Bhai Patel thought to be devoid of 'social value' and coined the term 'Socially Useful Productive Work' (SUPW). Its central purpose is to shift the centrality of education from excessive verbalism to practicality. It has raised certain academic questions apart from the availability of teachers and other resources.

Work education is a powerful medium for personality development. There can be a variety of activities which are necessarily school based and which may be included under work education like maintenance of the school plant including its playgrounds, cleanliness, repair of furniture and production of material to be used as instructional aids. It will be a great educational experience if community visit, field work, nature study, school co-operatives saving bank, games and sports and other co-curricular activities are carefully organised as part of the programmes leading to development of qualities needed for the success of work education.

TEACHING OF EDUCATIONAL VALUES

It is generally agreed that cognition is basic to volition which by implication would mean that prospective teachers are expected to understand critical issues regarding values—concept, types, and problems involved in imbibing the values. It is also expected of them to be well-versed with the values enshrined in our Constitution and the values that have the cultural contexts and can be derived from our heritage. In the process of capacity building of intending teachers, what is of importance is to ensure that they become capable of understanding the import of value education, interpreting values in the contemporary contexts and evolving strategies of imbibing these by their students.

An overview of the preceding details would bring in focus the duration required to transact the curriculum and ensure achievement of objectives of teacher preparation at this stage. Through the national consultations initiated by the NCTE, a strong consensus emerged in favour of enhancing the duration of B.Ed. programme from one year to two years.The new curriculum frame not only transforms the nature and content of the traditional foundation courses but also includes several additional components.

The practice teaching is now not merely confined to the teaching of certain subjects. Pedagogical analysis of the subjects offered for practice teaching has been made compulsory. The prospective teacher will analyse the subject before going to class and evolve a need-based pedagogy and transactional strategy. The teacher educators will now deliver model lessons of different types in actual classroom situation and the prospective teachers will not only learn the techniques but make its critical appraisal and evaluation to be subsequently discussed with the teachers. Teacher educators supervising the classroom performance, pupil teachers will discuss their observations with them for providing proper feedback to improve their performance. The practice teaching will, thus, require thorough preparation, detailed supervision and adequate time. Its gain would be acquisition of higher level of teaching competencies.

The practical work has been made comprehensive and meaningful. Internship programme shall be enriched to provide all the experience that a teacher needs. After completion of the period of internship the prospective teacher will acquire necessary experiences for working in school and the training received would be complete as against the partial one at present. The implementation of internship in this format will also need increased duration.

The field work, community interaction, school community relationship and similar programme will enable the pupil teacher to develop a need based pedagogy. The organisation of physical education and the educational activities, work education, sessional and practical work related to practice teaching and optional, the formulation of programmes for the development of personality, creativity and aesthetic sensibility and action research will lead to the promotion of skills and competencies needed for a teacher. The practical activities mentioned above will enhance the competence of the teachers. The duration of the B.Ed. pogramme will therefore have to be increased.

Besides these, a perceptible change in the pedagogy of teacher education itself has been suggested. Its centrality has shifted from the training colleges to schools and its transactional strategies have been transformed. The teacher educators have to make pedagogical analysis of the subjects to be taught and achieve integration between the theory and practice and also the methodology of teaching. They are expected to evolve a culture-specific and need-based pedagogy and develop the potentiality needed for independent learning and self study for which a number of suggestions have been made. The lessons will have to be supervised intensively and formative approach has to be adopted. The teacher educator has now to devote more time in the preparation and planning of his own activities for the professional uplift of the prospective teachers by developing certain additional competencies. All these demand more rigour and need more time.

Professionalism involves its own compulsion and pressure. It needs a change in attitudes and value systems of the teachers. They have to earn social sanction from the community by improving the quality of their work. The scope of teacher education has been enlarged. Teachers have to perform many additional roles in society. Apart from teaching, they have to act as the agent of change and modernisation, cultural reconstruction and social development to earn recognition as a professional from the society by acquiring new competencies and commitment. They have to become effective and result oriented to enhance their knowledge and develop skills for its communication. These are not possible to be achieved within the short span of one year.

Hence the need to increase the duration of the present B.Ed. programme from one year to two years. Existing programmes of two years duration leading to Bachelor's degree in education like B.P.Ed. may continue to be of the same duration. Two years B.Ed. programme will provide a strong base for pursuing M.Ed. course duration for which may continue to be the same as at present.

Teacher education programmes have to respond to three major determinants: the stage-specific developmental characteristics of the students, the courses of study they pursue and the academic qualifications the prospective teachers possess. At the Senior Secondary stage all the three become distinctly different from that of the secondary schools which offer a common curriculum upto class ten.

Teacher Training : Modern Trends

Teacher education with a view to making it relevant to the school system as well as training needs for preparing teachers at different levels will have to be further restructured, reorganised, and revamped. Multiple models of teacher education may have to be evolved by the universities and other agencies. The innovative models to be undertaken have to be relevant from the point of view of the teacher educator as well as those who will assume the role of a professional, requiring interdisplinarity, broader vision and goal consciousness and commitment. These would lead to the improvement in the standards of teacher education and develop professional competencies.

Another significant feature of such models would be their feasible and cost effective. The detailed course outlines will be developed by the universities through their various academic bodies. It, however, pre-supposes that the duration is suitably adjusted with the entry qualifications. Mis-matches between the needs of teacher education institutions and the professional preparation of teacher educators working in such institutions will have to be bridged. There are several workable propositions for evolving a variety of models like school based model, community based model, discipline-oriented models, integrated models, comprehensive models etc. Needless to say, it would be necessary to initiate integrated and comprehensive programmes of teacher preparation in both academic and vocational streams. The stage-specific and need-specific models will have to be evolved. These innovative models should be promoted and financially supported.

In-service teacher education within the overall framework of teacher development, has a crucial role to play. It is no cliché but a reality that those who teach should never cease to learn. The National Policy on Education in India, 1986 stipulates that teacher education is a continuous process and its pre-service and in-service components are inseparable. The initiatives taken in setting up District Institutes of Education and Training (DIETs), Colleges of Teacher Education (CTEs), and Institutions of Advanced Study in Education (IASEs) are some of the major developments in this regard.

Professional development of teachers begins with pre-service and gets renewed through in-service programmes. It, however, does not mean that there is a simple linearity between the two. There are elements of 'change' and 'continuity' in teacher education system which necessitate renewal and upgradation of skills and competencies. The in-service programmes are also organised to sustain the 'survival competencies' which the teachers acquired years ago, during pre-service education. In the professional updating of teachers, changes in the societal goals, educational structure, curriculum framework, transactional strategies, evaluation techniques and management processes play a significant role.

New advances emerging on the educational horizon have to be addressed to and teachers made aware of the same as well. Teacher development is a complex process. Teachers update themselves by putting in various efforts of self-learning, peer learning and interactions with the community. Other alternatives to professional development are participation in recurrent programmes, extension activities and continuing education programmes. In-service teacher education programmes are essential in view of obsolescence as well as explosion of knowledge and are necessitated on account of changes in educational and social realities.

Whenever teachers are required to execute new and different roles or get promoted to a position that requires new set of competencies, participation in appropriately designed in-service programmes is called for. Advances in the fields of curriculum, evaluation, audio-visual aids, telecommunication, etc. demand updating and orientation of teachers. Innovations both at macro and micro levels, would fail if teachers are not equipped and properly oriented to implement.

In the Indian context, the developments, such as the 10+2+3 pattern, the making of science compulsory upto class X, new practices in evaluation like internal assessment, question banks, continuous and comprehensive evaluation, scaling and grading, introduction of new areas like environmental education, population education, computer education, AIDS education, gender sensitivity, etc. demand in-service training of teachers. In-service training programmes are offered in various ways. Resource institutions at the national level offer orientation programmes of varying duration for different target groups. Besides this modality there are others like attachments, visits, national exchange programmes and international study visits; which form a significant component of in-service programmes. Pre-service and initial teacher education is reinforced by self-initiated learning, in-service teacher education programmes and recurrent and continuing education. Self-initiated learning involves study on one's own for professional development. Recurrent and continuing programmes are organised through seminars, workshops, orientation courses etc. as per the professional requirements.

In the changing context of globalisation, liberalisation and advances in tele-communication, teachers and teacher educators need to become conversant with international trends, internationalism, multi-culturalism, multi-racialism and other pluralities. Both pre-service and in-service teacher education programmes should be receptive to new thinking and new changes. However, reforms and innovations in education can reach schools in large magnitude and expeditiously through in-service education programmes.

In-service teacher education broadly perform the following functions:

a) updates teachers in issues concerning content, methodology and evaluation,

b) upgrades serving teachers in tasks with which they are currently occupied,

c) initiates and orients teachers to new roles and technologies,

d) provides opportunities for unqualified or underqualified on-the-job teachers to update and upgrade their knowledge.

While content, design and duration of each programme would be determined by one or more functions identified above, long range efficacy of any programme would also be judged by its impact on the following :

a) personality of the trainees ;

b) motivation and commitment in matters relating to professional and self growth ;

c) awareness of social realities; and

d) communication and evaluative skills;

In-service teacher education has to be organised for achieving the following broad objectives :

a) to upgrade the qualifications of under-qualified and/ or untrained on-the-job teachers.

b) to upgrade the professional competence of serving teachers.

c) to prepare teachers for new roles.

d) to provide knowledge and skills relating to emerging curricular changes - content, process and evaluation.

e) to make teachers aware of critical areas and issues, like, competency-based learning, multigrade, multi-level and multi-channel teaching, teaching students of disadvantaged groups, meeting educational needs of children with learning problems, developing inquiry skills, use of mass media in education, community participation and educational development of dyslexic children.

f) to overcome gaps and deficiencies of pre-service education.

In-service programmes need to be built around 'transform-ational objectives', i.e. increasing motivational level, enriching self-concept, building climate of inquiry and making teachers reflective practitioners. The thrust of transformational objectives is to develop such qualities in teachers as would enable them to become receptive, perceptive, reflective, innovative and dynamic.

Strategies adopted in in-service teacher education programmes would vary programme-wise and theme-wise. One has to judiciously select an appropriate training strategy or a mix of training strategies keeping in view the theme, programme duration, background of participants, availability of resource persons, support material and technologies of training at hand. Training strategies would range from lecture-cum-discussion to project work, library work, group interaction, field visits.

There may be many models of in-service training. Some of these are given below:

- *Face to face Institutional Model*: In this model, the training institution offers in-service training programme on its premises using direct face to face training approach. It is most effective when the number of participants is around 30 to 40. Besides lecture-cum-discussion mode many other transactional strategies are also used namely project method, case method, library work, peer learning sessions, buzz sessions, and small group techniques. The merit of this approach is that there is a direct and sustained interaction between participants and resource persons. The limitation of this approach is that it cannot be used when the institution wants to train a very large number of participants within a short time.

- *Cascade Model*: In this model number of persons to be trained is very large and training design is built on two or three tier systems. In the first level the key resource persons are given training. They train resource persons who in turn train teachers. The advantage of this model is that a large number of teachers can be trained within a short duration of time. However, it has its limitations. Knowledge and information passed on at the first tier of key resource persons and then at the second tier of resource persons get somewhat diluted resulting into transmission loss of training effectiveness.
- *Media Based Distance Education Model*: With the advent of satellite technology and computers many training programmes are imparted using electronic media. Audio-conferencing and tele-conferencing are already being used. In these the electronic media play the key role and print material play a supportive role. The advantage of this model is that training objectives can be achieved within limited time period. The constraint of this approach is the limited availability of the technology itself, and its high initial investment.

Besides the above three models, some other important considerations contribute to effectiveness of an in-service training programme.

- *Locale*: Training institutions at the national, state and district level organise training programmes generally at their respective institutions. These institution based trainings have their own strengths in terms of availability of resources. Their limitations are that they dislodge participants from their work place. This approach is often known as off-site approach. On the other hand using on-site approach many institutions organise training programmes at the school site itself.

Thus participants are not dislodged from their work place. Extension programmes and on-site programmes take training to the doorsteps of schools/institutions.

– *Target Groups*: At present in-service programmes are organised largely for teachers. A few programmes are also organised for headmasters, principals and other supervisory staff. This net has to be widened and many more categories of personnel brought into the fold. In-service teacher education programmes ought to be offered to all teachers working at pre-primary, primary, elementary, secondary and senior secondary levels. These could cater to teachers working in formal schools, non-formal centres, open and distance teaching institutions and institutions of physical education, adult education, special education, etc.

Teacher educators, in general, have limited exposure to in-service education. There is a need to train teacher educators at all levels. In fact, an apex institution needs to be set up for training of teacher educators. Alternatively some selected institutions may develop special expertise in training of teacher educators. Such institutions would have to develop relevant support material and undertake critical research studies relevant to in-service programmes of teacher educators.

Besides teachers, supervisors and administrators, there are other categories like Zila Pramukh, Pradhan, Sarpanch etc. connected with Panchayat Raj System who have the responsibility to look after primary level education. Depending upon the resources available staff of the support system, including librarians, hostel wardens, etc. should also be exposed to various programmes to enhance their professional competence.

- *Transactional Strategies*: An effective in-service education and training programme would use various transactional strategies like case study method, brain storming sessions, panel discussions, seminars, symposia, small group techniques, project work, library work and lecture-cum-discussion sessions. The organisers and the resource persons can make an in-service teacher education programme more effective and interesting if the age, experience and background of participants are appropriately used at the planning phase. Since in-service participants bring a lot of experience and way of looking at educational events, they can significantly contribute to the design and development of programmes.
- *Content*: Content of in-service programmes would depend upon objectives of each programme which could be grouped under the following major categories:

    a) school subjects.

    b) pedagogy and methodology.

    c) emerging issues.

    d) teacher's new role.

    The focus of in-service programmes is on developing competencies and commitments. The overall aim of in-service programmes is to enable teachers to improve their classroom activities, out-of-the-classroom activities, school activities and community activities.
- *Evaluation and follow-up*: Evaluation is a weak link in many in-service training programmes. In most of the cases in-service programmes are evaluated, if at all, on an ad hoc basis. Each in-service teacher education

programme should have monitoring as an integral component so that effectiveness of a programme can be properly assessed and apraised. Programme evaluation should assess whether the required inputs were provided to the programme on time, the logistics properly looked after and coordinated, the reading materials provided to participants etc. Another aspect of programme evaluation should be to assess the gains of each participant. The other subtle aspect is the impact evaluation to assess the impact of the programme at the grassroot level and in the field situation. Success of an in-service teacher education programme may be assessed by collecting perceptions of trainees and of resource persons.

3

Contextualising Teaching in Rural Primary Schools

Although all schools may suffer from constraints and problems such as those discussed above, the situation in many primary schools in rural areas is particularly difficult. Rural schools in developing countries suffer even more than their urban counterparts from the major afflictions of low completion rates and under-education of completers. This in turn results, in an under-educated adult workforce; the rural-urban divide is not merely maintained, but increased. There are examples of countries (Zimbabwe, Sri Lanka, Ghana, Colombia) where major reforms have been introduced in an attempt to increase provision of primary education in rural areas. These included curriculum reform, decentralisation of examinations, transfer of responsibility for some funding to community members, and changing concept of the teacher's role towards being a facilitator and even an entrepreneur.

Parents in rural areas may be very suspect of their children receiving an education packaged as "rural" which they perceive to be inferior to other aspects of the national education system, especially if it is thought to limit chances for future employment and educational progression. Socio-economic factors are also critical to the success of educational reform; regardless of changes in the curriculum which aim to relate learning more closely to the local environment, economic and social constraints in rural areas deter many of the poorest families from sending their children to school. More far-reaching structural changes in rural education may become necessary, such as adapting the school year of rural schools to fit more closely with the agricultural cycle, so that children who are expected to participate in agricultural activities will be able to do so without missing out on schooling.

The rural context is characterised by comities and, in order to analyse the situation further, it is useful to look at three distinct environments; the home, the school and the community. This can be illustrated as shown in Figure 1.

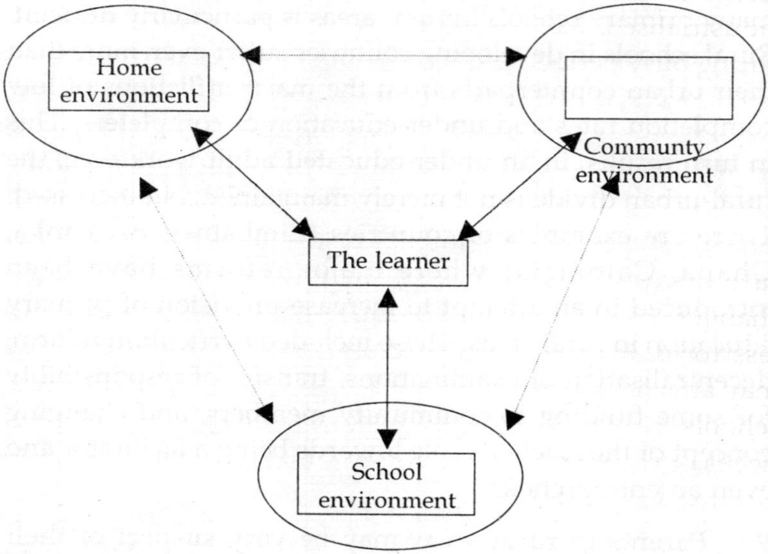

Key
Indluence/link
Weak or non-existent link

Figure 1. Linking school, home and community environments

It may be noted from this diagram that the linkages between the different environments may vary in strength. The learner is the common factor between all the environments and hence has strong links with each. The linkages between the environments themselves may be comparatively weak, however.

Home Environment

In rural areas, parental income levels are often low, and so financial contributions to schooling from nongovernment sources may be negligible. Children are frequently expected to assist with production-related tasks, and so are not allowed to attend school. Timing of the school day and of terms is often designed to fit more with an urban, industrialised system, expecting children to attend school during busy periods in the agricultural year. Large numbers of children in rural areas do not go beyond the primary cycle for socio-economic and geographical reasons and because of the urban focus of the education system. Thus there is a need for a system of education which would develop the learning potential of rural children and take care of rural needs in relation to resources and future changes. Parents in rural areas are likely to have received less formal education than their urban counterparts and may attach a lower value to schooling. Homes, and indeed schools in rural areas, are often ill-equipped to meet the needs of children to study; for example, with an absence of electricity. Children may come to school undernourished and in poor health, placing a greater stress on a single teacher who may have to deal with fifty-plus children ranging in age from four to fourteen years in one room which lacks the most basic facilities and resources (books, visual aids, etc.).

Disadvantaged children are characterised by a limited background of language and experiences in their home environments, resulting in difficulty in fully comprehending the language and the concepts used by their teachers, in books and in other materials. This lack of "relevant" experience often results in pupils not being able to think about abstract ideas. Those who were not very successful are likely to be less eager to learn, and hence a vicious circle is formed.

The term "disadvantaged children" may now be seen as somewhat pejorative, since it could be used to make a broader, unjustifiable inference about the value of a rural environment and culture from which a child originates. Indeed, many rural development practitioners now emphasise the importance and value of rural peoples' knowledge, and the need for rural education and extension programmes to build on it as a foundation. Seshadri talks of "shedding aside the patronising attitude towards the disadvantaged", and instead "capitalising on the strengths of these classes". The real issue to be addressed, therefore, is not the value of a rural upbringing, but the fact that the aims and processes associated with primary school education seem to be based on an acceptance of a certain range of knowledge, skills and attitudes, the acquisition of which is deemed as valuable and necessary for citizens of a "modern" society. Knowledge imparted within schools is seen by many as "superior" because it is part of a "superior" culture of civilisation.

School Environment

There has long been an ideological debate over the content and processes of education for rural children. Amongst some educationalists there is a belief in the existence of a body of academic knowledge which, although unrelated directly to the life experience of many people, should be learned by all:

"...the educational value placed upon abstractness...is a correct one, even though it also has a fetishistic element. It is also correct for schools to specialise in forms of thought which are not easily mastered through the informal culture. The critical thing is whether they present these forms as alternative or complementary to informal culture"

Cox and Jones suggested that there is a need to deliver the same basic skills to children the world over, since the ability to abstract and master the written word leads to the acquisition of the tools to exercise power, by mastering knowledge that is outside the scope of personal experience. Their view is that this conforms with what parents want for their children, i.e. the means of their children succeeding in finding well-paid employment. Coombes suggests that the "minimum essential learning needs" for children growing up in rural areas should include: positive attitudes, functional literacy and numeracy, a scientific outlook, and functional knowledge and skills for raising a family and operating a household, for earning a living, and for civic participation. This view would be supported by many. For example:

"The basic literacy and numeracy skills are of greater value than specific technical skills when students are unable to find work immediately after they finish training. Technical skills tend to deteriorate with disuse, and employers prefer literate and numerate recruits who can follow instructions and acquire new short-term skills quickly as new job opportunities arise....Primary and secondary school curricula must focus upon the basic skills of numeracy, literacy and scientific understanding".

Often associated with this type of approach to learning is a curriculum which is undifferentiated. In this case there would not be any radical difference in curricula experienced by children grouped according to some perceived disadvantage; any difference should be in the methods of presentation and teaching. The argument for this is that differentiation can result in segregation, and thus some sort of social stigma could be attached to the children, besides prematurely (and probably unjustifiably) closing doors to further educational opportunities. This could also accentuate the urban-rural divide which is observed in many developing countries, thus exacerbating an already difficult situation. Although this approach to primary school curriculum development and teaching is supported widely, an accusation has been levelled against it on the grounds that, in practice, such a curriculum tends to be geared to those children whose experience conforms more closely with a culture identified as "modern" and "superior". What makes matters worse is that the "superiority gap" is becoming accentuated, since the global influence of western media and marketing organisations increasingly interprets as "modern" a middle-class, urban dream-world, inconsistent with the reality of most rural communities.

Curriculum design is often centralised and rigid, revealing an urban bias and middle-class, westernised values, with no opportunity to relate learning to the situation from which rural children come. Children are not stimulated to learn, and rarely engage actively with the learning material. The learning material itself may be based on examples and situations which children in rural areas never come into contact with. Ekanayake believes that an irrelevant education breeds discontent and frustration and suggests that, in many instances, children who finish primary school seem to be less fit to be creative members of the community than if they had never been to school. He terms them "the schooled illiterates".

Ekanayake has highlighted a number of deficiencies relating to the school environment in rural areas. He notes that interpretations of children's problems are influenced by socio-economic determinants of achievement and pedagogical traditionalism, whilst the teaching styles prevalent today are the products of these social determinants. Because of this, teachers are unable to comprehend the irrelevance of the content and methods as the main cause of failure, high drop-out rates, non-participation of students, etc. Often, problems with children in the classroom and their intellectual progression are blamed on the home background and hence the parents. The teacher may be at fault, however, through not understanding the cultural background of the child.

As Ekanayake states, many teachers, due to their lack of training in rural pedagogy, are unaware of the poor quality and nature of academic support that parents can give at home. Parents often remain outsiders of the school system, students are passive listeners in the classroom and teachers are passive executors of predetermined curricula. The adverse situations resulting from deprivations are further aggravated by the fact that teachers begin teaching not with what the children know or have experienced but with what they do not know and have not experienced. This is because teachers have been presented with traditional philosophies of education which conceptualise parents as an important part of the learning process, so that if one part fails, so does the whole educational process. This reinforces Ekanayake's view that teachers lack skills related to effective use of the rural environment, knowledge of local culture and appropriate attitudes, and the ability to use the children's experiences at home for teaching and learning.

The importance of focusing on rurality as a policy becomes paramount, rather than as a matter to which lipservice is paid only.

Teachers in some rural schools are themselves from urban areas and have little or no understanding of the background of their pupils; they may be posted to a rural area against their will, have to travel a long distance to school and, as a result, may have very little commitment to their work.

As a result of demotivation, the curriculum implemented may vary markedly from the original, time available for learning is likely to be reduced, and pedagogical practices are likely to be poor. The teaching styles adopted by some urban teachers may be alien to what rural children experience in their day-to-day activities because these elite styles presuppose cognitive frameworks based on middle-class cultures.

Community Environment

In order to relate schooling to the community environment, some efforts have been made to integrate "community" or "rural peoples'" knowledge into the curriculum. This certainly has been one of the aims of the community school movement, yet it has proved a minefield, since an assumption was made, generally, that school and community knowledge systems are compatible. This led to the development of the argument that, since reality is socially constructed, knowledge which represents an interpretation of that reality or is based on direct experience must be specific to the society in which it develops. Consequently, the basis of school knowledge should be community knowledge.

To achieve this, some countries have developed and implemented a "ruralised", vocationally-oriented, diversified curriculum. Here it is argued that, in addition to literacy, numeracy and scientific understanding, children should acquire skills in technical areas which will relate directly to future work opportunities, particularly in agriculture. This has meant in practice that the content and activities included in the ruralised curriculum are related explicitly to the experiences of children brought up in rural areas. There is here, typically, some kind of focus on local, rural, social and functional issues, including the learning of basic agricultural skills. In this sense, such a curriculum may be relevant in two major ways, firstly in that the curriculum is relevant to the life experiences of the learners, and secondly that the learners acquire knowledge, skills and attitudes which will prepare them for life and work in the community from which they come.

Primary education of rural children is thus seen as having a vocational orientation. This type of curriculum may be quite rigid, but with a rural bias. Agriculture has often been an important element of the curriculum in these community-oriented schools. Where agriculture has been included as an intrinsic part of the rural schools curriculum, it has been implemented either as a manual activity, added on to the school curriculum, or as a distinct subject area in the curriculum. Primary school agriculture (PSA) frequently forms an important aspect of this type of curriculum, and, indeed, a great deal has been written about it, particularly by Bergman, Bude, Eisemon and Riedmiller and Mades amongst others.

A number of factors have contributed to the failure of many of these efforts to provide communityoriented schooling, however. As Bacchus pointed out, the integration of school and community knowledge is beset by an innate conflict between the two knowledge systems. He noted also that knowledge is not value-free, and is either used as an instrument of social control or domination, or as a tool for conscientising pupils. This view is supported by Bude:

> "....the school can either contribute towards deepening or fostering the apprehension of the cultural environment by endorsing its values for the socialisation process and thus by integrating cultural manifestations into the learning contents, or it can ignore or even negate these values and activities and thus accelerate the loss of cultural identity on the part of its pupils".

Attempts to integrate school and community learning have sometimes led to accusations of creating a strong class bias, providing children with the skills and attitudes needed to fill pre-destined positions in the community and thus fixing their societal roles. Some schools were accused of destroying the best elements of communal life and introducing a new set of values unrelated to the old one. Problems arose also due to a lack of major commitment by policy makers and funders, lack of proper training for teachers, insufficiency of resources and a poor response on the part of the public, who prefer more prestigious academic programmes.

Detractors of the ruralised, diversified curriculum believe that it leads to the creation of a dual system unwanted by parents and pupils, still failing the group of children who are most disadvantaged in society. Also, in most countries, a national curriculum is developed centrally; the inclusion of agriculture, for example, in a national curriculum might be to the disadvantage of urban children since it is likely to be outside their life experience.

Another enduring problem is that agriculture and other forms of technical skills training may indeed relate to the life experiences of rural children, but it is well documented that many community members, particularly parents, view primary education as a means of enabling their children to leave agriculture behind and to go to work in urban areas where they may earn money which can be brought home to the family. They do not want their children to be exposed to a "watered-down" version of the national curriculum which may prevent them gaining a fully-recognised qualification, thus impeding their chances in gaining employment or progressing to higher levels of the education system. Such a view could lead to parents withholding their children from primary school; hence there is a need to raise awareness that contextualisation can enhance the possibility for children to pursue and attain a wide range of goals in life.

Finally, there is the debate over whether vocational training in school, for example in agriculture, actually has any impact on levels of production in the community. White argues that acquisition of literacy and numeracy may be more effective than school agriculture in increasing agricultural production levels, and makes the case that school children should learn "about" agriculture, rather than "for" agriculture; the objective should be to promote "agricultural literacy", rather than to produce trained farmers.

Eisemon notes that learning about modern farming techniques in school does not appear to create better farmers once they return to the community, partly because the adoption of innovative farming practices seems to depend more on the level of cognitive development in an individual, and also because much of the technological content of "modern" agriculture bears no relationship to traditional agricultural practices and knowledge. As Eisemon states:

> "The content of agricultural instruction and its articulation with instruction in modern science is particularly important. Also important is connecting instruction in modern science and modern agriculture to indigenous knowledge systems, building upon the knowledge and skills students possess from social experience".

These problems have led many community school movements to revise their strategies. Most now aim to meet community manpower needs and to be involved in activities directly aimed at improving community life, for example by providing services locally.

Improved linkages between the school, parents and community and decentralisation of authority are important measures in moving towards a participatory environment required for improved learning. Some countries have already made this move in their constitutions. In Indonesia, the 1989 Education Law states that education is the responsibility of the state, the community, and the family. In China, the 1985 "Decision on Reform of China's Educational Structure" granted decision making powers for administration of primary education to local authorities.

Involving actively the community and parents in schooling, especially in rural areas where a large proportion of the adults will be illiterate, is an enormous task. It requires an enabling environment in which all members of the society - teachers, administrators, parents, educationalists - will work together in a participatory environment. Parental support is particularly important, as discussed at an EFA Summit of Nine High-Population Countries:

> "Women are the first and most important promoters of children's education. Their expectations and attitudes towards their children's schooling are an important factor

> in learning achievement. Research in several countries shows that schools which attain a high level of quality generally also enjoy a strong degree of parental support. Parents must feel that there are clear economic and social benefits in schooling their children, especially their girls".

Raising motivation and awareness in the community to the benefits of education, especially primary education, is a tremendous task. There is disillusionment with education when at the end of schooling, there is no job and no opportunities for progression to higher levels of the education system. Even within the community in which they live possibilities may be extremely limited, leading to the migration of many young, rural people to urban centres. Ram Niwas Mirdha suggests that the purpose of education needs to be better defined:

> "we should clearly say that it is not for jobs that we are giving education, but for providing you better tools for improving your situation - if you are a carpenter, you will be a better carpenter. If you are an agriculturalist, you will be a better agriculturalist with education".

Whether such an argument will improve public perception of education is open to question, however.

There is no doubt that linking school, community and home is difficult, but there is one common factor to all three environments which is the most valuable resource of all - the learner. In the various approaches described above, which aim to improve teaching and learning, little emphasis has been laid, explicitly, on the role of the learner in the learning process. Child-centred learning approaches have been advocated strongly for many years; an innovation which has sought to draw on this idea and develop it as practical application is the "child-to-child" approach to learning.

The child-to-child approach to learning is an interesting concept, and one that has been incorporated into many projects world-wide. It is evident that the high aims put on the learning expectations of primary school children are not met, and that the children leave school without the basic learning skills they need for a productive and progressive life. This approach follows the basic principals behind our approach for contextualising learning, based on a subject known to many rural school children. The child-to-child approach rests on three basic assumptions:

- that primary education becomes more effective if it is linked to things that matter both to children and to their families and communities;
- that education in school and education out of school should be linked as closely as possible so that learning becomes a part of life;
- that children have the will, the skill and the motivation to help educate each other and can be trusted to do so.

One particular study, analyses the child-to-child approach in the context of health education but emphasises that "such approaches to health education may help to "unlock" better approaches to learning on a wider scale". In other words the approach could be used to integrate or contextualise the curriculum. Hawes cites an example from a workshop held in Nyeri, Kenya:

> "child-to-child examined all the applications of mathematics to health and health to mathematics. They were legion. When we understand number, predict, estimate, measure, or solve problems we may do so in relation to imaginary cases (trains starting from different stations; A, B & C digging holes in the ground), or to real, important issues (population growth; budgets to feed a family; measurement of arm circumference). In the second

> case we do much more than teach interesting and relevant content at the same time as teaching learning skills. We also develop and reinforce the concepts and skills far more effectively because they are related to something both children and their teachers understand and value".

Child to child and child-centred learning approaches place the learner in a central role in the learning process. The learner becomes the core and focus of the entire learning process. The experience of the learner is drawn upon and used as a basis for the development of new learning. For young children, the home environment clearly is a crucial factor in their experience of life.

Many of the problems discussed above, such as those associated with socio-economic factors, are difficult to resolve since they cannot be addressed easily through educational reform, but require action by a wide range of stakeholders, including the government, local communities, and perhaps, under certain conditions, schools. Schools, presumably, can do something about educational problems. They do not hold the key to ali educational solutions of course, since government will need to provide complementary support by creating enabling policy and by supplying resources, not only material, but also through the reform of teacher training, learning materials production and curriculum development. Since a lot of what goes on in rural schools appears to differ quite markedly from what is propounded by policy makers and centralised curriculum developers, however, so schools may well be able to play an increasingly important role in meeting the needs of the children who attend them. As stated by UNESCO:

> "The school of today must overcome these developmental problems both in terms of relevance to the community and in terms of establishing a curriculum which is both universal and yet specifically tailormade for a particular situation".

In order to achieve this goal, the real challenge for a school is to strengthen and develop the links between the school, home and community. The learner can play a central role in this process, to the benefit of all. The "ideal situation" where learning environments are linked strongly. What can schools do in order to bring the learner into the heart of the learning process? In order to make learning more meaningful for rural children, it becomes necessary to create conditions where the curriculum and teaching and learning practices are influenced by the experience and environment of the pupils, enabling children to integrate their learning experiences inside and outside school. One innovation which may bring the different aspects of the learning environment together is the contextualisation of learning.

Implications of Contextualisation for Teaching

Educationalists have for many years been thinking about how the way children learn in school can be related to their environment. Gulliford and Widlake quoted John Dewey saying that,

> "Children are people. They grow into tomorrow only as they live today", and also "... when we say a child cannot understand, we frequently mean that he has not had sufficient experience of the right kind to be able to understand".

More recently, Bloom notes that children's:

> "personal experiences, emotions, metaphors, interpretative frameworks, and so forth serve to create a complex system of processes that affect the nature of their personal knowledge and how it is constructed".

From this perspective, the educational development of a child is inseparable from the "being" which the child has become, brought about through a complex history of social interactions and related to the context in which the child has been raised. As children develop, they continue to construct their own being, and education as an experience can affect and contribute to this process. This "constructivist" approach to the way in which children learn has challenged the Piagetian emphasis on individual cognitive development and is the subject of much recent research and writing.

Flick warns that any new instruction in school must constantly ask the pupils to re-examine past experiences. The analogies that they intuitively make must be explicit to them so that they can construct on their acquired knowledge. Linking past experience with concept formation through instruction is not a matter of finding the right analogy upon which to base instructional design, but rather the provision of a stimulus to trigger off other relevant experiences. Specific analogies can be used as a useful instructional tool, but teachers should be sensitive also to the spontaneous or intuitive analogies created by students.

Although everyday out-of-school experience contributes to the knowledge constructed by a child, additional experience must be provided within the school environment which will enable a child to understand complex, conceptual learning of skills in science, mathematics, languages, etc. In order to enhance a child's capacity to develop skills in these areas, however, it is essential to relate these subjects in some way to the child's own personal experience of life, and thus to integrate the entire learning experience. In order to meet the "essential learning needs" listed by Coombes, therefore, it becomes clear that the content of education programmes, the methods by which learning is facilitated, and the materials used to this end must all be pertinent to the experience and culture of the learners. In other words, learning should be contextualised.

The curriculum for rural primary schools in most developing countries is centralised and inflexible with an urban, western, middle-class bias. In these situations, decentralisation of the curriculum development process seems unlikely to happen in the near future. There are different approaches to curriculum development, however. Some educationalists advocate the creation of integrated curricula. Such an approach to curriculum development is certainly conducive to the use of contextualisation in schools, since there is much greater potential for teachers to develop the content themselves within certain topic areas. This means that they can relate learning much more closely to the local environment.

Bacchus defines integration as "the combination of the several components of an object, organisation or a system into a whole in order to render it entire or complete". A curriculum developed on this basis may have a core, which is identified as essential learning for all primary pupils throughout a country, but the way in which this core is handled is not prescribed by central policy makers. In order to render the curriculum complete, additional, optional areas will be included, depending on the locality of the school and the background of the pupils and teachers. There are strong arguments in favour of this approach.

As Krogh states: "Most of the learning in our lives is along the lines of an integrated curriculum". Following this idea, Krogh suggests ways that integrated learning, which prevails in everyday life, could be incorporated in the school programme. The teacher can choose a theme, create a topic web which relates and links a range of sub-themes or topics, and then add or subtract activities as it becomes apparent that there is too much or too little emphasis in some areas. This flexible method of teaching is an extension to natural teaching which takes place outside the school. It can build on a child's experiences, covering the whole curriculum whilst developing skills in a meaningful context, as opposed to breaking learning down into categories by subject area, which is less natural, more forced, and less interesting or exciting. Through a learning web, academic, social and emotional needs can be met. This approach was supported strongly at a recent conference held in Ethiopia:

> Children see the world holistically, that is they make meaning of their surroundings by making connections. Learning takes place through the introduction of new information which meets prior knowledge and experiences of the learners. Learners come to school with knowledge from their home, friends, environments, radio, etc. This knowledge is not necessarily broken up into maths, mother tongue, natural science, social studies, etc. They come with knowledge and experiences that have meaning to them. In helping children to learn new concepts and processes it is important to make connections to the knowledge and experience that they already have. These connections between new knowledge and their existing knowledge are best make in a holistic manner which is facilitated by the integration of fragmented subjects into one or two areas.

Most primary school curricula in use at present are not topic-based, but are organised according to the study of separate, specific subject areas or disciplines, such as language, mathematics, science, history, etc. Contextualisation still allows teachers to relate the content, however rigid, to the local environment. There are elements of all subject areas which can be contextualised. In this way, a centrally produced curriculum can be "localised" because teachers adapt the way in which they deal with the prescribed content by using the experience of the learners as a basis for teaching and learning. This is one way of addressing the problem of rigid "relevant" basic education programmes produced on a national scale, as curriculum flexibility is encouraged at a local level. The process of contextualisation will, necessarily, involve a range of stakeholders, not only school, government and community representatives, but also the learners themselves as they contribute actively to the learning process. An important impact of contextualisation, therefore, is, in the words of Lubben et al, "curriculum empowerment". Contextualisation can achieve the difficult task of linking "school knowledge" and "home knowledge".

Contextualisation can be applied in many different areas of the curriculum, but there are a number of implications for pedagogical practice. The size of the teacher's exclusive territory will decrease, inevitably, with a subsequent increase in the amount of input children have into designing their environment. This may pose a threat to teachers who are familiar with a strongly hierarchical school environment, and prove equally uncomfortable for pupils, parents and policy makers. Teachers will also have to develop skills in understanding the environment from which the learners come from, as their pedagogical approaches should attempt to "work in harmony with the world of the child and the community by, for example, including drawing, pictures, songs, stories and riddles of and by the local people and by encouraging the child to relate the content of the text to the environment often involving activities that would necessitate observation and analysis of the environment".

Many other types of inputs will be also of great importance, for example, the preparation of special materials, such as workcards, worksheets, additional pictorial or taped material, guides on the use of audiovisual materials, materials information and reference books which are easy to read in a language of instruction familiar to the children, whilst introducing novel terms in a suitably paced way. Lubben et al note that "contextualised materials stimulate student participation and provide the opportunity of identifying student misconceptions". They point out also that girls, who may feel alienated from schooling, can relate more easily to contextualised materials, and hence become more motivated to study and produce a better academic performance as a result.

Bearing in mind the severe constraints facing rural primary schools and teachers, a major difficulty associated with contextualisation is that its success will depend largely on the skill, motivation and professionalism of teachers, as well as the availability of suitable resources. Many materials and texts available currently are, as stated by Aghihotri et al "very distant from the environment of the child, both in terms of content and language". This leads to indifference, alienation and non-participation of the learner in the learning process. Another problem is that the experience, culture and "knowledge" of people who live in rural areas varies from one locality to the next; even within a specific area the knowledge and experience of individuals differs markedly. There is no single knowledge or experience which can be used as the basis for the curriculum, therefore. Metaphors and analogies should, if they are to be effective, be derived actively by the child, based on his or her individual experience and on experiences they may have in the future or which they find contentious or relevant for other reasons.

There are implications for teacher training, both in-service and pre-service, for more imaginative means of creating and distributing resources for teaching and learning, and also for time management, since the development of contextualised materials for teaching and learning will inevitably be a time-consuming activity. In this respect, it is important to be aware that many teachers carry a very heavy burden already; not only do they work under difficult conditions, often with large numbers of pupils, but they have to perform many activities relating to the social welfare of children in the school which go far beyond what is often thought to be the normal duties of a teacher. Ways of supporting teachers, both materially and psychologically, will have to be found which enable and encourage them to develop new strategies and approaches without becoming completely demoralised and exhausted in the process.

In order to contextualise teaching and learning, a teacher must identify aspects of the learners' experience which will provide a valuable resource of basic concepts, metaphors and analogies to which the content of the curriculum can be related. In rural primary schools, most learners have direct, first-hand experience of agriculture, either as a result of their own activities, contributing to the family livelihood, or from observation of their immediate surroundings.

An agricultural topic used as a medium for contextualising part of the curriculum could, therefore, provide an avenue through which children can have repeated experiences which help them to master cognitive, physical and social skills. Agriculture could be the basis of integrated projects incorporated in the school curriculum, with academic activities chosen for their locally relevant, experimental attributes. Even though the agricultural experience of individuals will differ, agriculture can still be used as a vehicle to make school learning more meaningful. Metaphors and analogies can be based on agricultural activities and experiences, and thus enhance the acquisition of literacy, numeracy and the skills of basic scientific reasoning within the confines of a subject-based curriculum.

Where the curriculum allows it, local agricultural practices can be used as a basis for "the development of an integrated life-centred curriculum with teaching devised according to "centres of interest" or "projects" where traditional subject boundaries are given up as artificial. During a period of several weeks, for example, all teaching would be centred around a given topic, with language, arithmetic and science skills being imparted in the process".

Children can be encouraged to relate the learning process in school with the natural learning process which exists outside the classroom, and begin to provide the means by which the process of learning becomes continuous, in school and beyond. It could enable children to develop not only basic knowledge and skills, but also higher-order competencies, such as problem-solving and thinking skills, and broader competencies such as leadership skills, group skills and personal initiative. This would be expected to enhance interest and thus motivation.

Coverdale suggested how a simple study of maize could be used as a theme for learning, whatever the structure of the curriculum. Measuring plots could involve mathematics, development of powers of observation and communication and the use of language. The history of the maize plant could be considered, as could geography in terms of where maize grows in other countries. This approach to learning aims to provide general education in an agricultural setting, since in rural schools, "there is a very strong case for a rural bias to be applied to the whole basic syllabus in order to give it a coherent pattern of meaning and relevance".

Agriculture provides an ideal basis for this "rural bias", because of its familiarity to the majority of rural school children. At home, many pupils will be involved in daily agricultural practices such as feeding and herding livestock, watering, digging and weeding. Agricultural seasons may also affect the pupils' school attendance record. This familiarity with agriculture may provide a basis for contextualising learning over a range of subjects, including reading and writing, mathematics, science, geography, social studies and home economics.

In order to adopt this approach, teachers would need to have an understanding of local agricultural conditions and also to have the capacity to learn from the local environment and from their pupils. As mentioned earlier, this has implications for teacher training and support. It would be necessary, also, for teachers to be able to produce learning materials which draw on agriculture as the context for the learning. Some school text books have been produced recently which encourage teachers to use agricultural illustrations for mathematics, science and languages; some examples are given in The Department of Primary Education, Sri Lanka advocate strongly the use of agricultural experience as a medium for contextualisation:

> "The success of the teaching-learning process depends heavily on the motivation of both the learner and the teacher. It has been identified that information regarding food habits and types of food of the community can be used in introducing innovative strategies in education. Outdoor activities using agricultural plots in the school and the home can also make learning more meaningful and hence attractive. These plots could be used for introducing concepts in mathematics, language and social studies, etc....Since agriculture is the main occupation of the parents in the Sinhala Medium areas, every attempt must be made to help them to learn better practices. Well maintained agricultural plots in the school could be used in teaching not only agriculture but also concepts in science, mathematics, nutrition, social studies, etc. These plots could also serve as demonstration plots for the

> community. In addition these could be used as nurseries to provide seeds and plants of improved varieties to farmers."

The use of agriculture in this way could have considerable advantages. It will appeal to parents and employers if it is proven that such an approach enables young people to cope more effectively with the subject matter in school. At present, passive, written examinations are the arbiters of success in most national education systems and this situation is unlikely to change in the near future. Although decentralisation of examination procedures is often discussed, many national policy makers still feel unwilling to introduce continuous assessment procedures which place new demands and responsibilities on teachers. It will be crucial, therefore, that parents and pupils feet that a new, innovative strategy introduced in schools will not reduce the chances of success in examinations; the aim of a strategy such as contextualisation is in fact to increase this chance of success, since by understanding abstract concepts better, pupils should perform better in examinations. Also, pupils who have left school should find that they are able to apply what they have learned in their local communities, and school pupils themselves will gain satisfaction from their own personal development. These skills will be useful, too, to those children who do succeed in progressing to higher levels of education.

The majority of curricula being used in primary schools are subject-based. A teacher will need to recognise, therefore, which aspects of the specific subject matter are amenable to contextualisation, by identifying elements which provide a direct link to the experience of most or all of the learners. This section highlights different curriculum areas which could be treated in this way, and pays attention, particularly, to the use of agriculture as a contextualising medium. As Riedmiller and Mades state:

> "The handling of regular school subjects is localised, by relating the topics of the separate subject syllabi to the local environment; in this way, the subject is the point of origin; the environment then functions as a teaching aid to illustrate academic themes and to serve as a practical ground for applying the acquired knowledge and skills".

One of the reasons that primary school children in developing countries appear to face difficulties with the study of science and mathematics is that the language of instruction is unfamiliar to them. Cleghorn et al describe, for example, the situation in Kenya where restrictions on the use of languages other than English during instruction may ultimately hamper student understanding of important concepts. When instruction is in a second language and when the concepts being taught lack equivalence in the students' language and culture, teaching involves a process of "dual translation".

Most cross-cultural studies in science education lean heavily upon the use of language to explore different meanings. This implies that cultural variation implies different ways of perceiving nature, and also, perhaps, that different languages directly affect how nature is understood. It seems to be the mother tongue, rather than the language of the school, which most affects the conceptual profile of children.

Children's language "turns inward" to become the basis of inner speech and so of thought itself. This is not a problem where the curriculum is taught in the local language, but there are cases where subjects such as science and mathematics are taught in English, French or Portuguese, and these are not the first language of the child.

Strevens made the point that most studies in the philosophy and the practice of science education embody two unstated assumptions: first that all the learners are members of the same culture, and also that they have the same common mother tongue. These assumptions are false in the case of developing countries. For example, in many rural schools, there might be different dialects spoken by teachers and pupils; there are cases when teachers have been posted to schools where a completely different language is spoken to their own. Another problem occurs when text books and learning materials are written in a different dialect or language than the "first" language of the children. Consequently, these pupils are disadvantaged in terms of language, not because their own is inferior or inadequate, but because they are required to conceptualise using words unfamiliar to them.

Strevens observed that the following problems were particularly common:

- unanalysed difficulties of mutual comprehension between teacher and pupil, especially in spoken English;
- the absence in the learner's own language of a word of expression equivalent to one in English;
- the absence in the learner's own language or culture, of a necessary concept;
- word-order difficulties.

Agriculture could provide a means of solving some of these problems, as the use of metaphors unfamiliar to the children constitutes an impediment to the learner's understanding. If the teacher allowed children to construct metaphors and analogies using their own language and based on their own agricultural experience, this could be an aid to deeper understanding of complex topics. Bude describes how children in schools in Cameroon use the medium of folk tales and fairy stories as metaphors and analogies, many of which are grounded in an agricultural context.

Cleghorn et al point out that when language restriction does not operate strongly in practice, as in the case of Kenya's rural schools, locally relevant examples are more easily brought into the lesson along with the occasional local term, hence meaning is better communicated. Children could also relate abstract concepts which are alien to their own culture through the medium of their experience of agriculture and local practice. Connections can be made between the concrete cultural world outside the school and the semantic organisation of the abstract world being constructed through science lessons.

Strevens points out that in many cultures measures are seldom exact, since approximation is more practical. In other cultures, weight and measures of weight are new ideas. The essential point, however, is that although a society and language may not employ concepts and terms that are identical with those of Western science, they will certainly have some concepts and terms which refer to number, measurement, agriculture, architecture, engineering, medicine, botany, and other fields of scientific activity. The cognitive task for the learner of science through English for example, is the acquisition of fresh attitudes towards observation and of terms for ideas which are partly new to him or her and partly just different from those already familiar. Agriculture can help to achieve a smooth transmission from one stage to another since new concepts will be incorporated in a familiar topic.

Agricultural practice in many countries is also closely related to beliefs which do not fit into a Western "logical framework", such as magic, superstition and ritual. There is now a recognition that much superstition is actually based on sound scientific principles, although not articulated in this way; a medium such as agriculture could help to identify the links between "modern" and "traditional" thought, demonstrate that these are not always mutually exclusive, and at the same time enable learners to understand scientific concepts and processes which are beyond their experience.

Cleghorn et al highlight one major problem associated with the use of local languages at primary school level. As a result of using local languages, it is thought that children may fail to advance quickly enough in the official medium of instruction. When this is an examinable subject, and even a prerequisite for promotion to secondary school, failure to read and write to an accepted standard could lead to drop-out, repetition and general demotivation. They note, however, that in rural Kenyan schools, using vernacular languages and terms to explain abstract concepts appeared to contribute towards literacy in the sense that children paid more attention to the topic, understood better what they read, and were therefore able to relate to it and better transform it to knowledge.

Combining the use of the vernacular language as a means to induce understanding, with English, may have expanded the children's awareness of word meaning and language differences, helping to develop their English competency while also fostering understanding of the concepts being taught. Their research seemed to prove that the use of the occasional local term assisted the process of moving back and forth between locally relevant concrete examples and the abstract. Since most agricultural practices, processes and concepts do exist in vernacular languages, this means that they can be used effectively to explain natural phenomena, and thus enhance understanding. Also, where agriculture is used as a basic theme in an integrated curriculum, learning will not be confined only to everyday situations, but will facilitate the acquisition of a wide range of skills, eventually helping school leavers to achieve social mobility, should they desire it.

Husen and Keeves describe a programme initiated by OECD with participation from UNESCO for the redefinition of curricula in the areas of science, technology and mathematics education from kindergarten through to secondary school in its member states. A characteristic of this changing educational scene is the greater emphasis placed on science education at the primary school level. In some countries this is a new development, so there is scope for seeking innovative ways of devising suitable curricula. The Nuffield science projects in the United Kingdom have aimed to promote thinking by children through the integration of science topics.

These developments were furthered as a result of the 1985 Bangalore Conference on "Science and Technology Education and Future Human Needs". The starting point for this conference was to identify issues that are essential for development, including food and agriculture, and to examine how science teaching could be developed without maintaining the division between the "pure" sciences, physics, chemistry and biology. This resulted in the generation of ideas and new techniques for science teaching at all levels on the themes mentioned. A meeting was held subsequently in Zimbabwe in 1990, which involved African teachers and curriculum developers, generating African materials for African schools on socially relevant aspects of the science they teach.

The inclusion of science in the primary school curriculum can provide an extremely efficient vehicle for teaching the skills of communication and of numeracy and for doing so in a natural integrated manner. Most important, however, is the concept that science teaching should be child-centred. Husen and Keeves point out that the way in which children solve problems is essentially a scientific way of working. School experiences need, therefore, to build on what children do naturally. Scientific enquiry is valuable because it helps children learn about their surroundings in a way which is natural and acceptable to them, by practical exploration relying heavily on sensory experience. Involvement and discovery help the child to communicate. Activity-based curricula can allow children to gain concrete experience of the world.

Agriculture can provide practical activities which are grounded in scientific processes. This relationship places the emphasis on the processes of science rather than the content. Agriculture can also provide a means of allowing children to develop, carry out and evaluate their own research projects; as a result, the nature of scientific enquiry is experienced rather than "taught". This can enable children to compare, analyse the benefits and constraints and identify linkages between traditional farming methods and "modern" methods. George describes how school pupils in the Caribbean study "modern" technology in order to develop problem-solving skills and to become aware of the social implications of the introduction of modern technology in a developing country, whilst at the same time recognising and developing the capacity of indigenous technology. Valuable work has been carried out also on the in-service training of secondary school teachers in Swaziland to enable them to develop and produce contextualised science materials. Through contextualised teaching and learning, children can develop their capacity for meta-cognition, and hence reflect critically on their own practices and experience; this may have a positive impact in the long run on agricultural innovation, production and rural development.

Just as development of science-related skills and literacy are important for children, so is mathematics. Yet it is probably the subject most frequently cited as being a barrier to advancement through the school system. Some governments actually make mathematics a non-compulsory subject area for promotion to secondary school or to further education. The result of this is that an individual can proceed through several levels of the education system without being numerate. University entrance criteria in many developing countries are based on the attainment of a qualification in mathematics, since this is the factor which lends itself most easily as a cut-off point in a list of potential candidates.

Balfanz considers how the mathematical knowledge children develop on their own, outside of formal school instruction, can be used to increase the distribution and level of mathematical knowledge attained by students. Clements and Jones described a case study from Papua New Guinea which detailed the learning processes of a child who came from a society which did not have names for numbers; still it was evident that there was mathematical knowledge in the society, but conceptually quite different to the standardised, western-oriented version. Damerow notes that social and cultural conditions are strong determinants of the acquisition of mathematical skills, as are the organisational structure of the school system and the nature of classroom practice and interaction.

Agriculture can play a role in contextualising mathematics, just as it can for science, since it allows children to conceptualise mathematical principles as they relate to experiences with which they are familiar. Even if their vernacular language does not have terms for numbers, agricultural examples could be used to draw on the meanings which do exist in that culture, and bridge the gap between the two knowledge systems. Instead of creating despair over the abstractness of routine arithmetic calculations, the recognition that mathematics contains elements familiar to the lives of children outside school can help to reassure them, and hence build self-confidence and increase motivation. At the same time, it was observed earlier that agriculture integrated into the curriculum can help to improve literacy rates, and this in turn should have a positive impact on the level of numeracy in children.

In order to achieve health for all, teachers must try to find ways to incorporate nutrition education more fully and effectively into the curriculum. She notes that successful teaching largely depends upon local initiatives and the level of co-operation between the school and teachers and the local community rather than implementing ideas produced by outside experts. It is unusual to find nutrition education as a separate subject in schools in any part of the world, and it is accepted, usually, that it should be incorporated into other subject areas. At primary level, nutrition education very often forms part of thematic studies which include literature, mathematics, history and geography as well as science. Agriculture, food, nutrition and health are, by nature, very closely related, and it should be possible to define themes which integrate agriculture and nutrition into learning experiences in other aspects of the curriculum.

Drama, poetry, music, art were included in the subject areas in which teaching about food and nutrition featured in addition to mathematics, geography, history, science and technology, physical education and home science. This approach was based on the use of the local environment as a basis for activities which encourages children to be curious about their surroundings, to observe, explain, experiment and communicate their ideas and findings. Turner describes the ways in which many primary school topics related to nutrition are frequently incorporated within a scheme which forms a part of an integrated programme of work and which includes aspects of health education and agriculture.

A study of staple food, for example rice, cassava, or bread could be based on a visit to a local farm, market or the school kitchen. Work in science and mathematics can be extended by germinating rice grains and measuring the growth of seedlings. Food can be integrated into studies of geography and religious ceremonies, in order to better understand social and economic factors. Children can then learn more about the complex interactions governing attitudes to food, and hence learn about agriculture at the same time. Activities related to school gardens or farms can also provide a rich source of low-cost, easily available classroom material.

Agriculture can be used as a means of preparing students to cope with sensitive biologyrelated social issues. The issue of birth rates and population control, for example, could be dealt with in an agricultural context by examining the impact of changes in the population rate on agricultural production systems; this combines social issues in relation to both agriculture and biology, hence facilitating a two-way flow of information and a build-up of knowledge of farming systems and biological principles within a social context.

Environmental issues are equally amenable to this treatment, since children have a wealth of environmental knowledge on which to base learning. Issue-based studies may help to sensitise young people to local development problems, bringing about a positive impact in the community. It may be possible to deal with gender issues in a similar way. Krugly-Smolska reports that it is important to begin the process of changing cultural stereotypes in children before they leave primary school. Since farming activities in many parts of the world are performed by women and girls, the relevance of the agricultural context may be even greater for girls than for boys, especially if they are active in the process of metaphor and analogy construction. This could lead to the development of greater selfconfidence in girls, and hence greater motivation to remain at school, helping to redress the problem of higher drop-out rates for girls than for boys at primary school level. Finally, Krogh points out that as children mature, it is possible to move from ego-centred social studies to a focus on the rest of the society. By integrating the theme of agriculture into the curriculum, a domain of personal experience for most children in rural schools becomes the basis for primary school learning; this may help children make the difficult transition from orientation towards the individual to an orientation towards society.

4

Operation Blackboard

For the last few decades, increasing efforts at the policy level are being made to combat the 'push-out' effect of primary schools, which in 1986 contributed to a drop-out rate of 52.4% by the end of the 5-year lower primary stage. Although children are successfully 'pulled in' or enrolled in schools, they are gradually pushed out again by a number of factors, many of which are directly school-related: an unattractive classroom environment, teacher absenteeism, teacher-centred teaching, low skill attainment, and a stagnant daily routine. The improvement of school facilities, under Operation Blackboard; the establishment of District Institutes of Education and Training; and Minimum Levels of Learning were all measures introduced in the National Policy on Education, 1986 to improve the quality of the school process.

If quality improvements are to happen, much depends on the ability of the system to resuscitate teacher interest, improve their motivation and commitment, and enhance their professional competence, for 'the quality, competence and character of teachers' are the most significant factors influencing the quality of education. Also, since primary teacher salaries account for nearly 95% of State-level allocations to education —a proportion that, in the strained economic circumstances, has almost completely edged out expenditure on other items—cost-effectiveness and the return to this investment is a crucial issue for policymakers.

The Package of Operation Blackboard

The NPE 1986 aimed for qualitative improvement in elementary education, the increased retention of children in schools, and a move towards a child-centred approach to education. The major policy plank to improve school quality was Operation Blackboard, a centrally sponsored scheme which laid down, for the first time, the minimum criteria of a primary school: two rooms, two teachers (one of them preferably female), and a set of 'minimum essential' teaching learning aids (TLA).

The TLA included a science kit, maths kit, tool kit, 45 charts, maps, children's books, balls—and a blackboard. All existing schools were to be upgraded to this level, and no schools should in future be sanctioned unless they fulfilled the new criteria. Teachers' receptivity to the TLA component of Operation Blackboard is important, since it signals whether broader attempts to improve the quality of the teaching-learning process are likely to be successful.

For, behind the inclusion of TLA in the package of 'minimum essential' items for primary schools was the policy notion of more learner-oriented teaching, placing the individual child at the centre of classroom process. This notion ran counter to current practice in many schools, where teachers, steeped for years in the 'textbook culture', and usually operating in a classroom bare of anything that would enhance teaching—including, in 40% of schools, even that most basic of aids, the blackboard—had become used to working in an environment that was highly unconducive to their enterprise. Adoption of TLA, with all they implied, would be a very major step indeed for many teachers, a radical departure from what had become the institutionalised form of both teaching and learning.

The absence of TLA in schools hitherto can also be taken as an indicator of the low awareness by the administration of the process of schooling—the quality of the interaction between teacher and child. For instance, Gujarat State had a clear policy regarding the two other components of OB: since the early 1980s, it had pinpointed the need to eliminate single teacher schools, since they 'weaken the elementary education system. Such schools remain closed when the teacher is absent'. By 1986, a third of the State's primary schools were single teacher schools, 97% of them in rural areas. The potential supply of teaching staff is ample: less so the budget at State level for financing their salaries, and hence the inability to fulfil the policy target.

For rooms too, Gujarat aspired to providing all teachers with their own room, but a similar gap between resources and policy is evident in the remaining target of 37006 rooms to be built as and when funds permitted. Yet the State had no policy or funding schemes for the provision for teaching-learning aids, which have been supplied haphasardly by District/Municipal Board managements as and when their own funds have permitted.

Operation Blackboard, conceived on the base of statistical evidence of the shortage of facilities in schools, did not seek teacher participation or consent on the nature or pace of change. Thus, while teachers had very little say in the provision of extra rooms or teachers, designed to alleviate classroom overcrowding and improve teacher-student ratios, their reactions to the new TLA, with their underlying policy message, would indicate their willingness and ability to adapt to the type of change policy-makers envisaged. It emerges from the case study that teachers' readiness to respond to change is linked to their training and professional status, motivation and attitude to their work, relationship with the local community, and the quality of preparation offered by the administration.

Quality of Teacher Training

Pre-service Training

There is a positive correlation between length of training and quality of teachers. By 1986 in Gujarat, only 2.5% of the teaching force in the State's Std. 1-4 schools remained unqualified (two thirds of that proportion being women); but the State has acknowledged its own 'weak' position with respect to the quality of teachers. Gujarat has always had elementary teachers with a low level of general education: older serving teachers may be non-matriculates (with 7 years of schooling) who have taken a single-year Primary School Certificate.

The current two-year Primary Teacher Certificate (PTC) allows students to enrol at about the age of 16, on conclusion of their Secondary School Certificate (SSC): entrants to training college in Gujarat are two years younger than in most other States where the requirement is completion of higher secondary certificate. The State recognises that raising the age of entry to PTC is both desirable and feasible, but has as yet taken no steps in that direction.

Although entry requirements have been raised, the low general knowledge base of entrants means that much time during teacher training is devoted to re-learning the contents of the primary syllabus; correspondingly little time is left over for introducing pedagogical practices. A low general knowledge base of primary teachers may impact negatively in various ways on their performance: they are less likely to invite questions since they are not sure they will know the answers and not to know is not compatible with the image of the teacher; questions are a threat to completing the syllabus on time.

Most teachers interviewed felt their PTC training was not suitable for the situations in which they worked, since training colleges have a strong urban bias: this despite five sixths of teaching posts being in rural areas. Pedagogical practices in training colleges, according to teacher interviews, indicated little change since 1970, when a national study reported that colleges in Gujarat used none of the 'demonstration method, assignment and activity method, supervised reading and model reading techniques' nor audio-visual aids used in other States to varying degrees.

Teachers felt that their trainers were not sufficiently aware of the realities of small schools with single rooms and no facilities, and hence did not offer strategies for working in such conditions. In the top-down system, where Gujarat implements the National Council of Educational Research and Training (NCERT) syllabus with minor local changes, this is a reflection of unrealistic nationallevel thinking, for in the NCERT's 1991 revised teacher training syllabus, multiple class teaching is still treated as an 'additional specialisation', defined as an 'area of interest' although a 1986 national survey had established that two thirds of all primary schools were single or two teacher schools, where multi-Standard teaching is inevitable. Although the NPE 1986 intended that 'as the first step, the system of teacher education will be overhauled', Gujarat's District Institutes of Education and Training did not come on line until the mid 1990s, long after the policy impetus for Operation Blackboard had worn off.

In-service training

When Operation Blackboard was launched, Gujarat had only very limited facilities for in-service training, provided sporadically by the State Institute of Education. The quality of this Institute, set up in 1969, was weak at a time when it played a key role in orienting teachers to the changes expected of them. Its capacity to perform as a nodal academic institution is doubtful, given that its academic staff comprises Readers who are exclusively ex-District Education Officers; thus although qualified to B.Ed. level, their recent practical experience is of secondary level administrative affairs rather than elementary teaching.

For most serving teachers, in the absence of institution-based in-service training or school cluster arrangements, visits by inspectors constitute the only form of support. This arrangement too is problematic: their role presently amounts to friendly policing of schools, rather than offering academic guidance and support to teachers; in the current structure, there is no opportunity for any professional training for inspectors. Also, although the official ratio is one inspector per 50 teachers, the ratio in practice is nearer to 1:90 in some Districts which means that inspectors find it very difficult to cover their beats. In-service support for teachers is therefore very limited: in effect, teachers do not have a proper channel through which to seek help with any academic problems they might face.

Professional Status of Teachers: Some Case Studies

The character of the primary teaching force has changed considerably since the introduction of a fixed salary and government service status, which accompanied mass expansion of elementary schools since the 1950s. Links with the community have often been lost, as, instead of being a highly respected member of the village community, a teacher is posted to a village to work in return for a fixed salary.

Primary teaching in particular is no longer dominated by upper-caste Brahmins, and has become widely accessible to lower social strata. The current composition of Gujarat's elementary teaching force includes 12.9% from Scheduled Caste and 15.3% from Scheduled Tribe communities; so nearly 30% of elementary teachers are drawn from what have been considered the 'weak' social sections.

Until recently, the rapid growth of the primary school network meant that a teaching post was virtually guaranteed on completion of training. Low entry requirements for a lifetime of secure government service are powerful attractions amid high levels of unemployment and 'diploma disease'. In recent years pay levels have been increased, but for many years low salaries contributed to making primary teaching an unattractive proposition, and to the low status of the profession.

There is little opportunity to grow professionally: avenues for career advancement within elementary teaching are very limited. Teachers may work in larger (1-7 Std.) schools, or move to the inspectorate or teacher training, where there are few places. For those who do opt for teacher training, there is no obviously suitable qualification since the B.Ed., the next level of upgrading for an elementary teacher, is primarily a qualification for secondary teaching. To combat the problem of teachers' unwillingness to serve in rural areas, Gujarat operates a bond system for new teachers entering their first post: they must complete three years' service there or forfeit Rs 10000, the equivalent of some 5 years' salary. There is a salary incentive of Rs. 40 per month for a tribal area.

While the bond system allows the State to 'solve' its problem of recruitment to the unpopular rural areas, and helps curtail the political machinations associated with teacher transfers, it does mean that inexperienced 18 year-olds can be posted to a community with which they may hardly even have a language in common.Teacher motivation and attitudes to their work. Among some fifty teachers interviewed across the three case study sites, only three really wanted to teach: for the others, teacher training was a relatively inexpensive route to a settled and secure life. This situation is by no means untypical on a national scale. Many factors weighed in teachers' motivation and attitudes to work, but one of the most important was their level of satisfaction with the place of their posting.

Teachers in Karjan

Karjan taluka is largely agricultural, and although it is considered by government officials to be relatively well developed, this development is uneven, with basic infrastructural facilities such as roads and pumps still lacking in the areas furthest away from Karjan town itself. The taluka's literacy rate corresponds exactly with the District average (then 44%). One third of the teachers interviewed were of Scheduled Caste, and all the others from general social groups; there were no tribal teachers. Almost all were native to Karjan taluka and were settled there with their families. Most teachers were in their forties; only one was in his late twenties and one was 56. No teacher was in a first posting. Almost all teachers came from agricultural backgrounds: their mothers were usually illiterate or had completed up to four Standards, while fathers had entered, if not completed, upper primary. They usually had some land holding which varied from four to fifty acres, and provided a supplementary source of income.

Only one had wanted to be a teacher; another was forced by financial circumstances to take up teaching; and one other mentioned an interest in giving to others. All others had been attracted by the ready availability of this job; the need for a secure income; and the possibility of working in their native place.

Teachers living in or near the urban centre of Karjan reported regular discussions on various topics with teachers and others working in the urban centre. Other teachers, who lived and worked in more remote rural areas of the taluka, had less opportunity for such interaction. Interviews pointed towards a correlation between teachers who sought closer contact with 'modern' life in the town, or even Baroda city, and an ability to exploit more widely the potential of textbook and TLA, representing an urbanised model of education, than those who were closely involved only in the 'traditional' rural sector.

Teachers in Karjan brought a mixed range of attitudes to the job and communities in which they worked, but overall the feeling tended to be positive. Teachers mentioned that 'teacher interest is most important thing', or they could 'identify with how children feel', and the importance of creating 'a loving and child-friendly atmosphere'. More than one teacher expressed pleasure at the opportunity to give to others; there was generally a sense of respect for the job and an awareness of the responsibility attached to teaching young children.

Teachers did not show much concern about the poverty of the school conditions in which they worked, and which Operation Blackboard sought to address. Since, in general, their expectations of teaching had more to do with their personal security than vocational ambition, they were not ambitious for change: they were settled in their jobs, and concerned to discharge their duty, but tended to have other side occupations, such as farming, in which they were personally more actively interested.

Teachers in Chhota Udepur

Chhota Udepur is one of Baroda District's three tribal talukas, and forms part of the long tribal belt of Gujarat, bordering States lying to the east. Characteristically, the hilly and remote terrain of the tribal belt is difficult to develop, and despite extra financial inputs under Tribal Development Plans, the State struggles to provide basic facilities such as roads and pumps. The problems are exacerbated by the traditional hamlet settlement patterns, with relatively small populations requiring expensive facilities. The tribal population retains to an ever-decreasing extent its own identity, reflected in its characteristic dialect and strong musical traditions. Economic conditions are often poor, and many tribal people migrate in search of labour work in cities, to supplement the meagre income from a single crop during the year.

The profile of teachers in Chhota Udepur was significantly different from that of Karjan, although an agricultural background and low parental levels of literacy were common here also. About one third were ST, one third SC, and the remainder of general categories. Non-ST or SC teachers all came from homes where the father had entered if not completed Stds. 5-7, and mothers had completed Stds. 1-4. Among tribal teachers however only one father had completed Std. 4 and otherwise both parents were illiterate; so all but one of the tribal teachers were first generation learners. Parental educational levels among SC teachers were higher: one had had a literate mother, and fathers had all attended, if not completed lower primary school.

There were two specific age bands of teachers: four teachers were in their late forties or early fifties; most of the younger teachers were aged around twenty. Seven teachers were serving in their first post and of those, only one was tribal and native to the area; others were non-tribal and mostly drawn from the neighbouring District. All tribal teachers had worked only in this tribal area although they had trained elsewhere. Teachers who were local all owned shared land which they worked with their family; one owned a small shop providing day-to-day necessities for the village. This gave them a sense of permanence: teachers from outside living in the same or a nearby village to the school had no such ties with their place of work.

As in Karjan, these teachers' reasons for becoming a teacher reflected the poor prospects of employment in rural areas. Only one had actively wanted to be a teacher, while others had taken the opportunity on advice, and because jobs were available. The inexpensive training and the security of a job after only two years was mentioned by several teachers, especially in the face of poverty at home. But it was apparent that, while 'general category' teachers had entered teaching for economic reasons, there were other factors affecting tribal teachers' choice. Their comments point towards a lack of awareness about possible employment options; and the lower career aspirations noted by Chitnis—implicitly indicative of their low status in the wider social hierarchy.

In this area, most teachers, whether from the tribal areas themselves or from outside, perceived the local socio-economic environment to have negative consequences for student attendance and performance: 'parents don't take care of children, they don't send them to school even if they promise to'; 'parents are illiterate and not aware, and they don't feel the child should be educated, they are more interested in having the child work'; 'tribal people aren't ready for change'. Only one (tribal) teacher phrased the problem positively: 'literate parents would help contribute to fast progress in school'.

Despite their generally low morale it was apparent that teachers, with one exception, did not think they would be physically or financially better off in another field of employment, and had strong family motivations for remaining where they were. Teaching was in every case except one a pragmatic choice based on a perceived or actual lack of an alternative. Here also, the paucity of equipment and general conditions of their schools did not appear to have a negative impact on teachers, whose primary considerations were related to their personal security, in return for which they carried out their duty as a teacher.

Teachers in Subhanpura, Baroda

Subhanpura used to be a village outside Baroda, but has now become a lower-middle class suburb. In the vicinity are several, good quality, private schools where better-off parents send their children; thus the government school draws children of domestic staff, rickshaw drivers, and others who cannot afford the private schools.

In terms of physical infrastructure, urban schools are generally better off than the District Panchayat schools, with adequate rooms, blackboards and limited TLA, as was the case in Subhanpura. In contrast to the almost exclusively male staffing of rural schools, almost all the teachers here were female, from backgrounds where both parents had completed at minimum of Std. 7. and, without exception, of a higher caste than the children attending the school—there were no SC or ST teachers. Two had a B. Ed., a higher qualification than that required for their post, but preferred the short hours and 'easy' work of primary teaching. None was working in her first posting and all were married and middle-aged or above; none of them would consider sending their children to the school in which they worked.

Their comparatively better physical conditions notwithstanding, all had low motivation for their work, citing reasons such as the lack of facilities in the school and the weakness of the children which, one teacher said 'inhibits my performance so I don't bother much'. Caste and class considerations played a major part in their outlook; and were exacerbated by the lack of any identifiable community with which to interact, and the seeming casualness of—often illiterate—parents who do not ensure their children attend school regularly. These teachers were not concerned about professional commitments, but interested in personal convenience: the schools were easy to reach, the timings suited their family commitments, they enjoyed the interaction with the other women on the staff (during which conversation about students or teaching was non-existent), and so on.

Socio-economic Environment of Schools

The socio-economic environment in which a school is located is a very important factor in shaping the attitude of the teacher and the quality of the educational process. Each different school has its own 'culture', which is likely to affect its capacity for absorption of an innovation. At one end of the scale, where the relevance of the urbanised model of education and the impact of the 'modern' world are low, the level of a school may be below the minimum required to absorb the innovation, especially if the innovation requires large, rather than incremental, change. Such were the circumstances in Chhota Udepur.

In Karjan, educational conditions had reached a level where schools did not have basic operating difficulties and teachers were better able to face the challenge an innovation would present. With their enterprise better understood, teachers had greater accountability to children and community, and increased motivation to attempt the difficult process of change. In Subhanpura, teachers again had low expectations of the children, and low tolerance for their inferior caste and class ranking: there was no sense of common purpose and accountability to children was as low as in the tribal area: the prognosis for adoption of an innovation was correspondingly lower than in Karjan.

Mass Orientation Programmes

The trends in teacher quality illustrated above are not uncommon all over India, and the extreme youth of teachers is an additional worry in Gujarat. How teachers of this calibre can be encouraged and trained to respond to innovation presents a particular challenge to those who wish to initiate educational change. Yet OB was formulated with very little attention to how the gap between teachers' current practice and the desired behaviour was to be narrowed: despite the centrality of the teacher in this programme and in realising the policy objective of enhanced educational quality, it included no teacher training component.

Attempts were made to plug this lacuna through the Programme for Mass Orientation of School Teachers (PMOST), a series of 10-day camps with 50 teachers at each, using modular basic orientation material. A basic problem was that teachers had to be oriented to a scheme which in the first two years of PMOST existed as hardly more than a policy suggestion: in Gujarat for example TLA kits did not begin to arrive in schools until 1988, the programme working its way through the administrative machinery, unseen by teachers, until then. There was a significant time lag during which 'awareness was created but on implementation there was no significant progress'.

A separate, specific Operation Blackboard orientation programme in PMOST format was set up in 1989, to improve teachers' abilities to use the TLA supplied under Operation Blackboard. In Gujarat, the State Institute of Education, charged with ensuring full facilities were provided at all training centres, had failed to ensure TLA kits were available. As a result training was held without the full Operation Blackboard kit in some places.

Teachers in Karjan, covered by Operation Blackboard in Gujarat's first sub-phase in 1988, did not participate in PMOST-OB, but received a three-day training at District level, from State Institute of Education staff and the inspectorate. This was intended as a practical orientation for teachers, to introduce them to kit items and how to use them. This training did not cover the underlying policy message of a change in teaching approach, and with that, the reasons why new TLA had been provided.

Some of the teachers interviewed had already had the 10-day PMOST, some had not, a haphasard situation that is explained by centrally set numerical targets which had to be filled but not exceeded; but others had had had no training at all. Teachers in Chhota Udepur, covered in 1989, had mostly had PMOST-OB training but in general had found that it difficult to follow. Its content did not seem relevant to their problems and often they could not remember how to manipulate the items. Only two of all the teachers in this group had understood why it was necessary to adopt a change in teaching approach, and how the TLA could assist in helping children to learn more quickly, and with greater interest. Since the 'trained' teachers had not understood the training well, they had not passed it on to the second teacher, as the PMOST format had intended.

In Subanhapura, one teacher had received general PMOST training, but had not passed it on to other teachers as she could not see its relevance to their situations. For these teachers, there was a vast time gap between the policy orientation and the arrival of the TLA, since the kit did not arrive in the urban schools until at least three years after the policy orientation programme. Dorasami, evaluating PMOST in Karnataka, found that it 'did not help teachers develop a clear perception of the salient features of the policy' and that it 'made no impact on curriculum transaction in terms of utilising varied techniques in teaching'. Other available studies, such as those by Ramadass in Pondicherry and Acharaya in Gujarat, support these findings.

Teaching Learning Aids

Incremental rather than rapid change has been identified as a positive variable in connection with teacher adoption of an innovation. To be adopted by teachers, Operation Blackboard would need to build on some degree of teacher acceptance of a need for TLA. Prior to the scheme, some teachers had perceived a need for at least some type of simple TLA in the core subject areas and had tackled the lack of any teaching material by providing their own: sticks or stones for counting in both the rural and tribal area; and also home-made charts and other limited aids in the rural area only. In the urban location, nothing at all had been provided by teachers. For some teachers, therefore, Operation Blackboard was an incremental change, while for others, it was a much bigger step.

Although administrators had adopted purchasing procedures, which left something to be desired in the quality of teaching aids, the TLA in tribal and rural locations were, in general, usable. Teachers' responses to the introduction of TLA varied very widely. Almost all teachers used Operation Blackboard charts and leaders' photos to decorate the walls of the school. The abacus was usually to be found on top of the cupboard used for storing registers, while other TLA were in boxes neatly piled on top of each other and kept at one side of the room.

Teachers in the tribal area used virtually no TLA except the charts. The tool box was, justifiably, condemned as useless—of such low quality as to be unusable, in a badly deforested area. But most teachers ignored most of the other aids: when questioned more closely, it was apparent from what they said that some teachers had not even looked into the boxes to find out what they were.

Rates of usage were on average higher in Karjan, the rural area. Again, charts were universally adopted. The second most popular item was the abacus because 'students themselves can count' and the coloured plastic shapes because 'children can learn shapes and colours by playing'. But teachers had differing opinions about when aids should be used. Teachers who had not understood the policy message of a change in teaching methods felt that items were more useful in upper Standards only, as children should concentrate on learning reading, writing and numbers in their first two years. This seemed for them to preclude the use of TLA, for which children were 'too young'.

Other teachers felt that using TLA had benefits which embraced both teacher and child by making teaching and learning more interesting and thus more effective. Some teachers spoke of the monotony of teaching prior to Operation Blackboard, and the difference they saw in the children's interest after introducing a visual element. Two rationales given by teachers were: 'children are bright and if you give them material they will grasp fast.

Operation Blackboard can really broaden the range of activities'; and 'it takes less time to teach, it is practical and gives students life skills, things they can do at home. It used to be boring, now it isn't, the playway approach is possible and it's interesting. The economic problems haven't gone away but the intellectual problem is solved through playway teaching'. In the urban environment, implemented in 1991, the Municipal Corporation failed to deliver any charts and the Operation Blackboard items were of very poor quality. But teachers anyway consigned the kit to the cupboard without even opening it.

In designing Operation Blackboard, the Centre had required State governments to amend existing accounting procedures which hold teachers personally liable for repairing any damage to articles logged into their Dead Stock register. This wish was not complied with in Gujarat, but very few teachers seemed concerned about their Dead Stock register and potential damage to items. If a teacher was inclined to use TLA, s/he would do so regardless of breakage potential: 'if it breaks, it breaks, children need these things'. Those who did not adopt more TLA than charts were motivated by factors other than fear of financial penalty.

Charts were universally popular, except in the urban school where they had not been supplied. Easy to use, they quickly found a regular place in school activities: it was obvious to teachers how and where they could be used, since they fitted in with the textbooks. Indeed, it may be argued that the chart is little more than the extension of a textbook page and the adoption of this particular aid therefore follows naturally in a textbook culture.

Most of the remaining TLA were more complex and required some explanation and training as to how and why they should be used. Their 'training' left most teachers dissatisfied. Those who had attended PMOST had understood the stress on a changed role for the teacher; and that the object of Operation Blackboard was child-centred learning. In practice they had established that it is 'easy for a child to understand if there is a visual image'. Although teachers found their training had been carried out quite well it had been, for more engaged teachers, unsatisfactory because it was 'difficult to grasp fully within 10 days, and the lack of revision afterwards makes it easy to forget'.

Tribal area teachers who had attended PMOST-OB all felt that ten days was insufficient to learn the mechanics of using the items and how to relate materials to the child and teaching. The training did not appear to tackle the problems they faced in their daily work, which made the message of PMOST-OB seem irrelevant to them; but it unintentionally provided teachers with an opportunity for general discussions. These had focused not on Operation Blackboard or child-centredness, but on their difficulties with the local environment and the syllabus. These teachers are concerned that, because of language and attendance problems, they have great difficulties in completing the textbook (and de facto syllabus) in time.

They generally meet with limited success in their teaching of tribal children, which they explain in terms of the backwardness of the local community, the language problems and the lack of parental support for children. They dealt with these problems by adopting an attitude of 'they can't help it and neither can we'—a carefully balanced equation by which they adjust to their circumstances. PMOST-OB presented numerous challenges to this precarious balance: tribal area teachers were not receptive to Operation Blackboard because it was not felt to address what they perceived to be their most pressing schoolrelated problems.

In the camps, teacher trainers tried to persist with the unsuitable PMOST-OB material, since they did not feel they had the autonomy to adapt it to local circumstances. They held it to be their duty to impart training according to a prescribed format, the question of relevance being left to those who write the curriculum: 'The environment of the teacher is the biggest problem but we can't do anything about it because it is an administrative problem. The syllabus is designed to teach them and not to solve administrative problems'. In all areas, teachers who did not participate in an organised programme were at a disadvantage since peer teaching had largely not taken place: this could not be easily rectified since negligence on the part of the State Institute of Education meant that the Operation Blackboard kit itself did not include an instruction manual.

Teachers Attitude and Adoption of TLA

In Chhota Udepur, teachers tended towards a negative perception of the children they teach and the communities in which they work. Whether tribal or not, teachers are largely isolated from the local community, from whom there is usually little understanding of their enterprise. One teacher summarised a feeling apparently shared among outsiders serving in this environment: 'If the language isn't the same and the people are different, how can the teacher be expected to be there?'.

Tribal area teachers hardly looked beyond the problems they themselves perceived to think about how a child might find school, and in general did not connect the quality of the school process with problems of drop-out or non-attendance. They saw a connection between learning difficulties and local environment, notably irregularity and that 'students who want to work are hindered by the language problem'; but focused on how it affected themselves rather than its impact on the child's experience of school. Among these teachers, teaching was just a job: the lack of identity with the local community and apparent hopelessness of their task provided no motivation.

In Karjan, most teachers identified to some extent with the children they taught and were sympathetic to their problems. In general they were aware that using TLA would be beneficial to both themselves and the children, and had sufficient motivation to make some effort. Even so, the potential for increasing retention of children in school by enhancing the quality of the teaching process was explicitly realised only by one teacher, who said 'Operation Blackboard things make the school attractive, which is useful for children who don't like school. They can look at the things to gain interest and this helps to make teaching more practical; and it helps in creating a classroom atmosphere of love'—the latter he felt to be the most significant contribution a teacher could make to retaining a recently enrolled child. Otherwise, some teachers noted that retention had picked up when Operation Blackboard was implemented; and they felt that children were more attracted to attend school since Operation Blackboard, and the chance of working with different objects in the classroom. Urban teachers were all of a different caste and socio-economic background from the children who attended their school. All teachers mentioned that the children are low-caste and backward, with uncaring parents. They held these factors, about which they can do nothing, to be responsible for students' poor school performance, and for their own low motivation to teach.

At policy level, Operation Blackboard was intended to improve teachers' working conditions, and to enable them to transact the curriculum more easily through a more visual style of teaching, Among teachers who did not really understand the policy intentions, the attempt in this direction was seen as an extra and not as a solution to any of teachers' difficulties: 'most of the time we have so much work for language and maths that we don't get time to use the Operation Blackboard kit'. Introduction of TLA was not successful in amending many teachers' belief that the only function of a school in the first two years is to teach a child how to read and write, using traditional rote and blackboard methods. Only one teacher felt that he had really changed his teaching methods as a result of the policy initiative.

Operation Blackboard for Policy Implementation

The centralised, top-down approach to educational innovation implicitly assumes that the elementary teaching force is a homogenous body; and that the same centrally-devised package of equipment will be suitable for all teachers and all schools in rural areas. The inherent concept of a school is a well-ordered environment in which teachers would like to make teaching interesting for children, set in a 'modern' world where there is a place for books, where people read and write. But the reality of many schools in Gujarat, a relatively advanced State, is that children attend irregularly and do not sit still; and teachers are not concerned about whether their teaching is interesting, or even whether children learn, but how to complete the textbook on time.

The pedagogical problems of the teachers in Gujarat's rural schools are not primarily related to infrastructure, but to the absence of skills to cope with either teaching several classes simultaneously, or the needs of first generation learners, compounded by heavy and often irrelevant curriculum. The type of pre-service training they receive does not equip them with adequate classroom management strategies, or the confidence to adapt the curriculum, and is an important factor in low teacher motivation.

Despite their limitations, PMOST and PMOST-OB had raised teacher interest; but for less motivated or able teachers, this was not sustained by the system once they returned to their schools. For tribal teachers in particular, the gap between what was projected in the training modules and the known 'reality' of schools was too wide to be bridged. Those who devised these modules pitched the level of their content too high for many teachers, who in consequence derived little gain from them.

As a national policy innovation, Operation Blackboard lacked any element of motivating and supporting teachers. This reflects the centralised, bureaucratic administration of education, which maintains a large establishment but fails to attend to those central to its effective functioning. Everything that teachers have to do is laid down by a higher authority, which does not consult teachers on any issues however teachers might be affected, and makes no concessions to local circumstances. The lack of any consultation with teachers about the contents of the OB kit, and the failure even to inform them that the kits were going to arrive before they landed on their doorsteps, are cases in point.

Although the TLA were designed to help teachers, it appeared to many of them that they would add to their workload. Most teachers had not become sufficiently clear about either the theoretical or the practical reality of the change expected to make any adjustment to the way they teach. The majority of teachers interviewed showed no critical awareness of the relationship between their pedagogical practices, conditions in schools, and teaching problems. Some teachers understood teaching as imparting the content of the textbook, regardless of whether children learn.

In some schools, where children who had attended for four years could still neither read nor write, teachers did not accept responsibility for this situation and blamed the local environment: they did not feel that their own pedagogical practices required attention. In just a small handful of schools, teachers and children seemed to be working together with some sense of common purpose. Such teachers were able to make use of more of the items provided and to vary their applications: they saw relevance for TLA at all ages and not just after children have learned to read and write by using traditional methods.

As a result there was the least gap between the policy world and the 'reality' of school life. These schools are nearest to operating in the conditions where Operation Blackboard could make the difference policy-makers expected. But in these more favourable conditions, the composition of Operation Blackboard was such that it did not allow teachers to move far from a teacher-centred style of teaching towards the childcentred approach recommended in the policy. The TLA kit contained only a single set of items, so only the teacher can use them and not give them to children individually. Although aids were used, they were embedded in a flow of teacher talk, and there was no evidence of any move towards children asking questions, experimenting or manipulating objects without very close teacher supervision.

Adoption of an innovation is also conditioned by teachers' perceptions of policy. Ups and downs of government allow policy to be seen only as a political programme, rather than as a blueprint for the direction of change: 'Whatever government comes, we're concerned with education: if they change policy we'll work on, it has nothing to do with government'. Many teachers felt they were fighting a battle with a government that formulates policies that bear little relation to their situation: The government doesn't know what our needs are. The government makes policy for a city environment and in the villages the scene is very different. These city-oriented policies just aren't suitable for the village environment.

In all the case studies described above, teachers, in general, exercise any critical insight into the relationship between their teaching methods and the children's ability to learn: they are not reflexive practitioners. It is clear that many teachers do not view teaching and learning as a process: rather, teaching is a matter of imparting a set body of knowledge that students should learn to repeat without error. Some teachers do not feel responsible for what happens in the classroom: many of them are in the profession because it offers a secure income with short hours, it is available to those with low qualifications, and it allows a side business or family commitments to be facilitated. However, despite generally low levels of professional competence, many teachers are concerned to discharge their duties adequately, and are prepared to make efforts to improve their work, providing that both the reasons and the ways to do so are clear.

At present, there is little incentive for them to improve their performance. Teachers are little more than powerless subordinates in a bureaucratic hierarchy, conveniently available to be called on to discharge any government work that needs to be done at the village level. This robs them of the chance of developing any professional identity, and is a major barrier to improving the quality of the schooling process. The system 'dehumanises' teachers, and it must be prepared to amend this to allow the focus on human interactions in the classroom to emerge. Until this is changed, and autonomy is returned to teachers, there can be no expectation of an improvement in the quality of classroom process. The case study also illustrates that teachers need to be motivated to build good relations with the village or community in which they work, since this will provide one of their major sources of support.

Given these characteristics of the teaching force, the prognosis for any innovation which requires change in teaching practice is not hopeful unless it contains a large element of motivation and support for teachers. Cosmetic 'training' such as the PMOST programme does not answer their needs since the level it aims at is, in general, above that which teachers can respond to. Teachers often reported that they had forgotten much of what they 'learned', indicating that a brief once-off programme has little meaning for them; it is therefore also a waste of financial resources. The case-study indicated that teachers are willing to use TLA when they understand how it will make teaching and learning easier—for instance the visual aids, which were a near universal success. Charts also worked because they represented an incremental change, since teachers are used to handling text with pictures in the format of a textbook: transition to a chart was straightforward.

At the national policy level, when conceiving any innovation, the capacity of teachers to respond to the proposed change should be realistically assessed, in terms both of teachers' professional competence and educational levels of the communities in locations where they are likely to be posted. It must be faced that in many places, levels of both are low: both policy aspirations and teacher training inputs need to be adjusted accordingly.

Building on the issues which PMOST has introduced, in-service training via the District Institutes of Education and Training should now seek to consolidate teachers' understanding of the theory of child-centred, activity-based teaching behind the policy innovation, and the practical uses of the TLA which are now available in most Std. 1-4 schools. Such training will be most effective if it is a continuous process with repeated, clear inputs aimed at a level that is within reach of the trainee. It may take a number of such inputs to bring trainees up to the level of the overall policy input, but anything less is a compromise that will be evident in practice. Induction into the special educational needs of non-mainstream communities and ways in which these can be met must also form part of District-level training; this should also comprise education on the particular problems facing first-generation learners in village and urban contexts, and how teachers can most effectively support them.

If teachers are to be motivated, and policy is to be brought into closer correspondence with their capacities and expectations, they need to be involved in decision-making about matters that affect them, not totally excluded as is customary. At present, teachers do not relate to policy as something designed for them; they see it as a political whim, and they are thus disposed, in general, to ignore it. Facilitating such dialogues, and thus bringing administrators, policy-makers and teachers into correspondence with each other, can become a regular activity of District Institutes of Education and Training, providing they seek to adopt a more holistic view of the whole process of education than the Primary Teacher Colleges they replace.

Te administration also needs to look to its own procedures to ensure that it too it doing everything within its capabilities to support teachers in what is, without doubt, a difficult job. Special emphasis needs to be given to the role of the inspectorate, so that teachers feel that someone both notices and cares about what they do, in contrast to the neglect they suffer at present. Thus, through an informed consideration of primary teachers' abilities and capacity to respond to the type of change proposed, and the circumstances in which change is to take place, policy-makers would be better able to set an appropriate pace and means in the search to fulfil the objective of universalising primary education.

5

Training for Teaching Science and Mathematics

Observations of teachers in their daily work in classrooms indicate a consistency between how teachers go about their work and their views of learning. This has been recognised through research and is described as teaching style or approach. One teacher will prefer to provide a range of activities for children, perhaps covering the whole curriculum, and will give the children a considerable amount of responsibility for choosing and completing their work. Another will keep the class as a whole for most of the time so that they will share the maximum amount of the teacher's attention. Yet another may encourage groups to work together and expect a cooperative product in some appropriate form.

When asked about why they choose one approach rather than another, the reasons teachers give are in terms of their views of what they want children to learn and what they think is the best way of helping children to learn it. Each conscious decision about how to arrange the class, what kinds of activities to provide, how to bring children into interaction with them aterials supplied, the kind of help the teacher gives and how success is to be assessed, will be consistent with the teacher's view of what and how children should be learning. For example, suppose that a particular teacher's view of learning is that it is a matter of rote memorisation. This teacher will provide learning experiences which expose children to accurate facts and encourage them to memorise procedures and algorithms. To do this efficiently the teacher will probably provide the information in digestible packets, each to be mastered before the next is attempted. The class will be arranged to optimise exposure to information from the teacher, from the blackboard and from books, and to minimise interference from non-authoritative sources, such as other children.

he teacher's role will be seen as being to ensure attention, to present information clearly and to reward accurate recall; the pupils role is to attend, to memorise and to recall; resources may be used to illustrate applications of facts already learned or just to add interest and prevent boredom. Of course, the evaluation criteria will be defined in terms of how well the children can recall or reproduce information. This teacher will be doing a good job of rote teaching; all the classroom conditions are consistent with rote learning and support its implementation.

If the teacher has a different view of learning, along the lines suggested in the Introduction and described in more detail below, where the learner is active in creating understanding and in testing and modifying initial ideas, then the classroom provision consistent with it will clearly be quite different from that described for rote learning. Now the experiences provided will enable pupils actively to seek evidence through their own senses, to test their ideas, to take account of others' ideas through discussion and using sources of information; the class organisation will facilitate interaction of pupils with materials and pupils with pupils; the teacher's role will be to help children to express and test their ideas, to help them to reflect upon evidence; the pupils' role includes some responsibility for learning and taking part in generating ideas; the materials have a central role in providing evidence as well as arousing curiosity in the world around. The assessment criteria must include reference to developing and using skills and ideas and not neglect the development of related attitudes.

Model for Classroom Decision Making

The model below is an attempt to convey this relationship between the kinds of learning experiences teachers try to provide for their pupils and the kind of learning they want to bring about. Their decisions about implementing this, in terms of the role they take as teachers, the role they allow for the pupils and the way in which they use resources, are made so as to be as consistent as possible with the intended learning experiences.

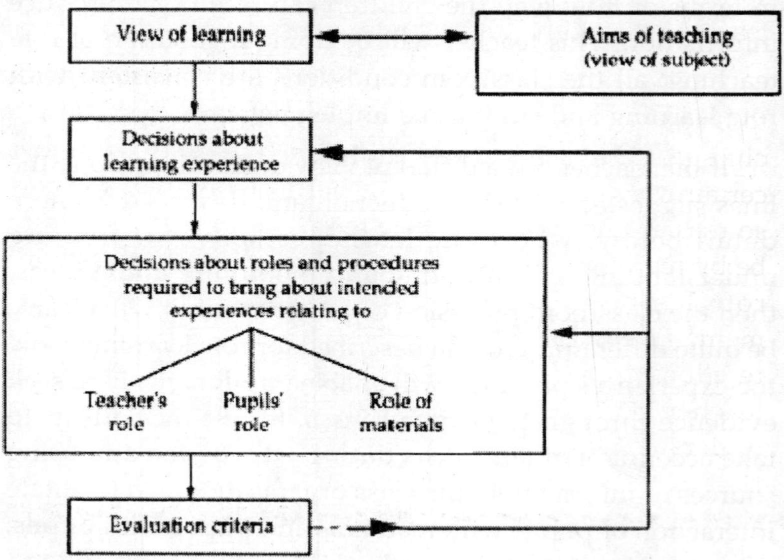

Figure 1. Model for classroom decision making

The success of the teaching and learning is judged against criteria which in turn are related to the view of what should be learned and how it should be learned. Feedback from evaluation brings the planned experiences and their implementation more closely into line with the kind of learning intended. The classroom of the teacher who values rote learning and that of the one who takes a constructivist view would clearly be very different learning environments. Assuming that we do not favour rote learning, a question for in-service teacher education is: how can we turn the first one, arranged for rote learning, into a different one, perhaps more like the second? At this point we must admit that we have ignored the inevitable constraints on teachers imposed by conditions such as class size and the provision of materials and basic facilities, which are not available to all teachers. Where teachers lack the conditions which would enable them to teach in the way they would like, the solution has to be sought through other channels than teacher education.

However, if the teacher is free to choose and has chosen to teach by rote, the answer to our question about how to change the learning environment (s)he has created is certainly not by telling him or her to reorganise the class so that, for example, the children sit in groups. Nor will it be by merely providing different books, since a devotee of rote learning can turn anything into an exercise of memorisation. What is required is for the teacher to become re educated as to the nature of learning. Only when the teacher is convinced that rote learning will not lead to understanding and is equally convinced of the value of children taking an active part in their learning will he or she be prepared to make the effort to organise the class, the materials, and to make the time, for children to learn in a way consistent with this view.

Determining the View of Learning And Teaching

The above model proposes that the views of learning and of the subject are the keys to the learning opportunities that a teacher provides for the children. It therefore follows that these views must be given a high profile in teacher education. The major question in the present context is: to what extent are the views of learning relevant to primary school mathematics and science the same?

Let us consider the constructivist view of learning as an example, first taking its application in science and, later, in mathematics education. This is a view of learning which holds that the learner, in trying to make sense of new events or objects, begins from relevant existing ideas or models and tests the extent to which the new phenomena can be explained using these existing ideas or models. If predictions based on a related existing idea or model fits the new observations, then the range of application of the idea or model is extended; if the evidence does not fit the prediction, however, this may mean that the idea or model has to be modified or rejected in the light of the new evidence.

Science encompasses the first-hand use of physical and mental skills to generate and test reliable knowledge and generalisations. In learning science, these skills are involved in using and testing existing ideas. It is through processes such as observation, questions raising and hypothesising that ideas are used in trying to explain new evidence; it is through processes such as prediction, planning, experimenting and interpreting that conclusions are drawn as to whether the ideas fit the evidence. If these process skills are not carried out in a rigorous and scientific manner, then the emerging ideas will not neces sarily fit the evidence. Ideas may be accepted which ought to have been rejected, and vice versa. Thus, the development of ideas depends crucially on the processes used. While the facts or data and generalisations are important, how we come about them and what makes us believe them are of equal importance. It is important that they derive directly from the phenomena themselves, that careful planning, observation and recording are done, and that the conclusions drawn are bases for further investigation and verification.

It follows that attention needs to be given to the way in which children test out their ideas in primary science, that is, to the development of the process skills. However, this cannot be done effectively by direct teaching any more than the understanding of abstract scientific concepts can be taught directly. Experience of attempting to give instruction in observation, or prediction, as such, using content-free activities (meaning trivial content, since there has to be some> is that the skills are not transferred to use in scientific enquiries as hoped. The usefulness of the skills in helping understanding has to be experienced. So a pupil who recognises that finding a pattern in observations has helped in making a useful prediction is likely to try this in another situation because of its value in helping understanding and not just because (s)he knows how to do it.

The on tinualinter weaving of knowledge and process skills in the investigation of natural phenomena is an essential characteristic of science education. Science also involves using the knowledge that has been generated through process skills to create and continually refine testable models of nature that help us to describe, explain, predict, and to conceptualise observable phenomena of nature. In this model building of science, the approach is first-hand enquiry built around experience and experimentation and the focus is the phenomena themselves. The models at first will be approximations that are improved or revised or discarded in the light of additional data that comes available as children's experience expands.

Children, like scientists, must be ready to reject ideas when the evidence requires this. In this way ideas gradually change and develop to be more encompassing, more generalised and more abstract. In the type of learning just described the learner collects the evidence and does the reasoning; makes the ideas his or her own. This is what we may call learning with understanding. Learning without understanding, as in rote memorisation, does not require the use of process skills. Learning with understanding helps children to feel at ease with science, to know its strengths and weaknesses, to realise how ideas emerge from human activity, which is important in their education even if they are not destined to practise science.

In mathematics education these same arguments apply in relation to developing children's knowledge, say of arithmetical operations, and to developing skill in selecting appropriate operations, knowing when to add and when to subtract. Children are often taught to know how to add, subtract, multiply and divide, but may still be unable to decide which to do when faced with a real problem.

Without experience of taking part in the construction of an algorithm in solving a problem the procedures have to be learned by rote, without understanding. They lack the understanding of what the process means in real terms and the ability to move from a verbal description of a problem, say of dividing a sum of money equally between a number of people ,and the appropriate mathematical algorithm. As in science, the aim in mathematics education is to stimulate and support learning with understanding. The interweaving of knowledge development with process skills and the resulting creation of models of the nature of things are elements that we believe should be at the centre of science and mathematics education.

This, then is the kind of learning which we aim to bring about in children through the education we give the teachers. To do this for teachers already in schools, through in-service education, it is often necessary to produce a quite radical change in their view of what teaching is and how children learn. This will not happen quickly or without some considerable effort on the part of those concerned.

The status quo acts to moderate attempts at change and to establish new patterns and move to a new status quo takes a matter of years rather than the months over which in-service activities are usually spread. In the case of teachers in initial training the position is not so different, since these aspiring teachers will have spent up to 12 years in school through which they will have developed quite firm ideas about teaching and learning which may well have to be changed.

So, because of the existing ideas and experiences which teachers or student teachers bring with them, in teacher education we are concerned with changing ideas, not just planting new ones in virgin soil. Producing change is notoriously difficult. In the context of curriculum development it has been a matter of concern since the early days of curriculum projects, in the 1960 s.

In the 197Os, Kelly and Rudduck and Kelly carried out studies of implementation of innovation in which they distinguished between trans location (just getting new materials to teachers), communication (getting a message over), implementation (using the new materials) and re-education (developing real understanding and commitment to the new approach embodied in the materials). Their work has been followed by many other studies which have shown that producing materials and ideas alone is not sufficient to change practice and that this cannot be done without the active participation and cooperation of teachers.

Problems in Science and Mathematics Teaching

Most of the points made above, although illustrated in terms of science and mathematics education, apply qually to most other are as of the curriculum. In science and mathematics, however, particular problems are encounte red. Many, perhaps most, primary teachers have received from their own education a legacy of failure or at least dissatisfaction in relation to science and/or mathematics. Thus their overriding requirements are for confidence, an appreciation of the nature of scientific and mathematical activity and enthusiasm for teaching the subjects.

These pervading aims have implications for the conduct of a teacher education programme, since they concern attributes which cannot be engendered through specific content but only in the way of dealing with that content (which may mean, for example, not lecturing to a large group of students as the predominant style of a course). In meeting these needs it is as important not to do certain things as it is to do other things. For instance, it would seem important not to teach teachers the science and mathematics background they need in the same way as they were taught previously and which dismally failed. Neither should we underestimate the value of their everyday knowledge, which may be implicit, rather than explicit, but could be greater than assumed. Further, we should not treat them as if they had no existing ideas of their own about teaching, learning and about the subject matter to be taught.

Mathematics and science suffer from the popular perception that they are difficult, remote from the understanding of most people and only for the 'specialists'. Teachers, as members of the society in which these views are embedded, tend to share these perceptions. They stand, therefore, to benefit from actions which are taken towards creating a more positive popular attitude to wards mathematics and science. More positiveattitudes of teachers will influence the perception of these subjects by their pupils, the future citizens, and thus break into the present vicious circle in which un confident teachers pass on their negative attitudes through the way they teach. Thus the moves to popularise mathematics and science are to be welcomed.

For example, a study by ICMI has provided both general considerations and concrete examples around the notion of presenting mathematical ideas of various level of sophistication to a wide audience. A further problem particular to science and mathematics is that the majority of primary teachers in most countries are women. Like many women, they have suffered from the 'masculine image' of science and mathematics. By this is meant the reputation these subjects have of being 'cold and calculating', objective, concerned with facts and accuracy, impersonal and excluding emotions and feelings. Such characteristics do not, as a generality, seem attractive to girls, leading to a high rate of drop out and a sense of failure and alienation from these subjects. Many theories have been put forward to explain this situation, relating to the psychological origins of personality, in born differences in spatial ability, social conditioning in early life, etc.

A growing body of opinion is looking at the nature of the subjects and the way they are portrayed in schools, rather that at the supposed deficiencies of girls, for the source of the problem. It has been suggested, in the case of science, for example, that "process-based science is likely to project a more human view of science and to involve learning experiences that engage the thinking, imagination and interest of pupils as well as leading to an understanding of key concepts and principles. The aim of this approach is for pupils to learn with understanding, through development of their own ideas, which are taken seriously and not ignored in favour of the 'right answer'. This type of learning is more likely to appeal to all pupils. "The same may be said of mathematics. If such a view of these subjects could be transmitted in teacher education it could play an important part in generating the confidence and enthusiasm which so many teachers lack. The importance of not reinforcing old prejudices follows clearly from this.

Science and mathematics are, after all, two distinct disciplines, each having its own characteristics. Using the word ' discipline' in close association with 'disciple' gives it the meaning of 'gathering information' or, rather, 'a process of building knowledge'. 'Knowledge' is then taken in the sense of a framework, or network, of interrelated concepts or ideas. The difference of obtaining and processing concepts an did as distinguishes the resulting bodies of knowledge, in this case science and mathematics. The distinction, however, does not erase the obvious relationship between the two disciplines. Consider some examples where the two ways of gathering knowledge run together.

Mathematical Problem in a Scientific Context

Children take a daily measurement of their growing maize plant. However, over the weekends the school is closed and no measurements are taken. How much did my plant grow on Saturday? How much on Sunday? This is now a mathematical problem. Keeping careful daily measurements on the weekdays, enables the children to employ the mathematical skill of graphing these, so they can interpolate the most probable lengths of the plants on the weekend days. Alternatively they canuse their measurements to calculate an average rate of growth, and use this per diem proportion to figure out the un measured magnitudes.

Scientific problem in a Mathematical Context

Where would my maize plants grow faster, inside the classroom or outside in the garden? An experimental situation as suggested by the question should be set up. Measurements need to be taken at regular intervals, both inside and outside, and the quantitative results compared. For more accuracy the daily rate of growth in both situations may be calculated and compared. For still greater accuracy a number of plants may be grown and measured, inside as well as outside, and average results may be determined and compared.

As these examples suggest, science often provides a framework, or context, for mathematical activity. The primary teacher who teaches the children both subjects ought to be aware of this, not so much from the point of view of designing a curriculum of mathematics, but in order to be ready to jump at every good opportunity to make the children apply their mathematical skill and knowledge in a situation of reality which happens to be meaningful to them. This places the children in a situation where they need and want maths. It enlivens the exercise, and provides sound motivation, for it carries within itself the reward of satisfaction. Mathematics is often called 'the language of science', for it enables the young as well as the older scientist to generalise, to summarise and to communicate in clear and concise mathematical terms, formulations and equations.

This is a great asset, and one more reason to insist on letting the children grow and develop in this most useful subject and apply it wisely. This simply means: teach the children mathematics with integrity and science with integrity. Instead of attempting to integrate what in essence stands apart, the two subjects are to be presented in a working relationship of interdependence where this is relevant and useful. In this way they become a most powerful educational 'tool' giving meaning and depth to the expression 'science and maths education'. The use of mathematics as a toolkit for science makes it by no means subordinate to science, and certainly not when one considers that everybody's science would be severely crippled in its progress without mathematics.

Mathematics deals with quantities and magnitudes which are specific properties of physical objects and materials. Whereas mathematics systematically loosens itself from the bedrock of concrete, physical objects and their quantitative properties in order to pursue pure mathematical patterns and laws in the abstract regions of numbers, spatial relations and algebraic structures, science keeps returning to the reality of physical objects, their interactions and working systems. The flight of a scientist into mathematical abstraction is always related to some physical, down-to-earth, concrete, matter of fact observation, which poses a problem and asks for understanding.

Archimedes shouted 'EUREKA' because he found a mathematical construct to express (and find) the specific gravity of materials. Thus he could distinguish the specific gravity of the metal from which the king's crown was moulded. By comparing the magnitudinal properties of the pieces of matter Archimedes used a mathematical way to come to a reliable scientific conclusion with regard to the quality of the king's crown. His prediction was based on mathematical insight and physical experience. Returning to the primary school, we find children who are taking their first steps in orderly scientific investigation.

The essence of their scientific activities is 'encounter and interaction'. Children encounter real objects, living or non living, which by their colour, texture, shape or behaviour invite or challenge the children to explore and investigate. This interaction between the children and the object of their immediate attention may be free and exploratory, but it can soon be given order and system by good science education when a good suggestion given by the alert teacher turns the free exploration into a purposeful investigation, whereby the children are encouraged and helped to develop and employ various scientific process skills.

Observation, questioning, trying to explain, or hypothesising, predicting and verifying by experimentation, are readily mentioned as typically scientific process skills. However, quantifying data, measuring and related calculation or computing, belong to the category of scientific process skills, too. These, by nature mathematical activities, are now applied to the solving of scientific problems. Certain scientific challenges call directly for specific mathematical activity, which provides a motivation as well as an opportunity to initiate and develop, through practice, these mathematical skills.

Developing Quantitative View

Developing a quantitative view of the world around is an objective of both science and mathematics education. This 'quantitative view' induces children (and adults) to find ways of measuring or otherwise quantifying things whenever this helps to solve a problem or whenever it would reveal some (new) relationship.

The mathematical requirements of the young primary scientist may be simple and straightforward, the necessary skills must well be mastered before any creative use can be made of them. Primary mathematics must take its own flight into more abstract working with quantities and magnitudes simply because it has an educational value of its own. It offers a different, if not a wider, context of application than science.

Training for Mathematics and Science Teachers

Children learn best when they occupy themselves fully with the 'things' that make up the subject of their learning. In science education these 'things' are real, concrete, touchable living and non-living objects or materials which are found or placed in a variety of situations. It could be a seedling growing on blotting paper and another one growing in soil. It could be a magnet picking up pins. It could also be a small community of living organisms growing, or moving about on a square metre of ground at the edge of the garden or somewhere in a piece of wasteland, or it could be a mealworm in a box given a choice between heaps of sand, sawdust and cornmeal.

In mathematics it could very well mean the same things, but then in some quantitative relationship on a slightly more abstract level: e.g. the daily rate of growth of the seedlings; the number of pins the magnet picks up; the measuring of equal distances between the mealworm and the three heaps of its choice; or the different sets of living things found within the 'minifield', or their coordinates for placing them on a map. But even if the 'things' of maths occupying the children are of a more abstract character, such as the symbols they use for numerals and signs of operations, or the planimetric figures they draw, these are still a self-created reality with which the children work.

In occupying themselves with their subject matter, be it the very concrete things of science, or the partly abstract symbols of maths, children go beyond mere encounter. They enter into a 'dialogue', an interaction with the object of their immediate attention, and they mani-pulate it in such a way that it reveals something of its own essence. This may be a property, or a 'way in which it works', or a sequence of 'things I can do with it', or something that has been uncovered, or that has been invented or even re-invented.

The 'revelation of something of its own essence' is nothing else but the formation of a concept in the mind of a child. This may be a new concept altogether, or some change or refinement of an already present concept.It could also be the rejection of some preconception which is now suspected as false. Finally, it might be a new association with some previous concept(s) so that a relationship is established which deepens understanding and insight.

The teacher who wants to engross the children in the subject matter of science and mathematics through real things and representative symbols which the children can handle, must himself haveundergone, or undergo, the excitement and joy of learning, and so share it with the children. Only then can the teacher appreciate a learning situation, assess its value, judge what next step should be taken, create new learning experiences, and foresee where the renewed investigation can lead.

Foreseeing what a learning experience can lead to implicates aninteraction of the teacher with the subject matter at hand on the level ofan adult, someone who has learned, through experience and study,

— to place a new concept in a wider framework of existing knowledge;

— to use a familiar concept in the wider context of one's (own) existing knowledge;

— to retrieve an old concept and to see its relevance in a new situation.

With this more mature intellectual potency the teacher can approach both the subject at hand and the querying, learning children, and so interact with them, being sensitive to their needs or wants, and helping them with word as well as with deed, so that they can see relationships and understand an explanation. The teacher's interaction with the children and with the subject matter may assist the children to recognise and make use of a relationship which they had learned already, so that they find or discover their own explanation of what they were puzsling about, or gain a new insight.

Now we can summarise the tripartite interaction which is in evidence in good education:

— The childinteracts with the'subject matteiathand (e.g. germinating seeds, darkness seeking woodlice, an isosceles triangle, or some quantity to be divided). At the same time thechild interacts with the teacher who with word, deed, or other intervention (or, indeed, by just leaving the child quietly alone) helps the learning.

— The 'subject matter' (which, broadly taken, comprises the 'stuff to be learned', the things to be handled, the sources being tapped, and the problem situations into which the children are placed) interacts both with the children to whom it presents a challenge, and with the teacher to whom it once was, or may now still be, a challenge.

– The teacher, in turn, interacts with the querying children as well as with the object of their query, namely the 'subject matter' at hand.

It is with this triple interaction pattern of education that we should seek for what teachers of primary mathematics and science ought to know in order to be good and confident in their teaching.

Knowledge

The word 'knowledge' does not simply represent a clear, unambiguous and unequivocalconcept. By different people, or indifferent circumstances, it may be given various shades of meaning. Popularly stated we distinguish:

– *A 'How-is-it-called-knowledge'* which relates mainly to the formulation of factual information, the right name, the appropriate word.It helps to show that you know what you are talking about, yet does not guarantee it. Learning by rote tends to lead to this form of 'knowledge' and go no further.

Because this aspect of knowledge is easily assessable, it may be associated with what is referred to as 'school knowledge', and as such be given undue desirability. Yet we should not underestimate the value of 'communicating knowingly' as it creates permanence in one's own mind as well as intelligent intercourse among communicating humans. Perhaps we ought to refer to this aspect of knowledge (which for a great deal fills our intellectual 'archive' called 'language') as 'social knowledge' since it covers words and terms, conventions and rules, established and agreed upon by society, which we can only learn by social contact with others by word of mouth or, otherwise, in writing. As examples one could mention: 'Naming the parts of the flower', or 'Naming the internal and external features of the frog'. Nomencla- ture is an obvious example. In mathematics one could think of the names of counting numbers, the names of geometrical figures, or of algebraic symbols.

— *A 'How-i~dppears-fo-be-knowledge' which* refers to direct experience.It is a knowledge emerging from interaction between an observer and the object under observation. It embodies properties or observable behaviour of real objects and their possible or actual interactions with other objects, or with the observer/learner. It is checkable knowledge, based on experience, observation, experimentation, research, induction. This makes it also changeable knowledge, adaptable, in as far as it can be adjusted by new experience or investigation, revealing new evidence. Therefore, it is often imperfect, biased, open to discussion. It may also possess a certain degree of probability.

  This knowledge makes 'prediction' possible: it stretches ahead, When you see lightning, you can expect a thunderclap; when multiplying any number by two results in an even number. Since the evidence supporting this knowledge is searched for in the physical world—in the nature of things as they are—it may, perhaps, better be called 'physical knowledge'.

— *A 'How-does-it-relufe-knowledge'*. This conception signifies a higher order of abstraction in which relationships between concepts become evident: generalisations, conclusions, and patterns inferred from repetitive experiences or experiments. It may also be deduced from pure thought processes in which existing concepts, at various degrees of abstraction, are related to each other, orare recognised as related to each other. Even reflecting on such thought processes may form new knowledge which, in the sense here elaborated, comes close to being identical with 'insight' or 'understanding'. A better name to indicate this knowledge would be: 'logical knowledge'. It is at this level of knowledge that we talk of insight and understanding, because it has been 'processed' to fit into a person's total store, or 'web' of acquired knowledge, beyond pure experience undergone at first hand.

– A *'How-if-should-be-done-knowledge'* which comes close to an ability to do things. However, it goes beyond the physical ability or skill in as far as it incorporates not only the remembered sequence of operations, but also the foresight to create, to invent, to lay out, and to plan a succession of processes or operations in order to compose things, to put things together, to calculate, to compute, to programme, to experiment, or to run an investigation. It has to do with algorithms, with rules of thumb, with safety precautions, with operations, physical as well as mathematical. This knowledge precedes skills and abilities, and motivates to do the necessary exercise to acquire these. One could call this 'technical knowledge' but then in a more than purely mechanical sense. Above the levels of imitating and the grasping of procedures one needs insight and inventiveness in order to be able to organise an experiment or an investigation. Resourcefulness belongs to this aspect of knowledge.

– *Finally there is a 'How-to-find*-your-way-about knowledge which makes a person resourceful enough to tackle any problem in the most effective way possible. It consists of a knowledge of resources and their accessibility. It is the knowledge of how to makeuse of any level of existing knowledge within oneself, coupled with the knowledge of where to look for and obtain the new information, advice, or resources one needs. One knows where to look for things, situations, people, books, scripts, charts, maps, archives, tables, computer ware and whichever other modes of storing information may be useful. This is the knowledge which leads directly to self-reliance in searching and in learning.

It should be emphasised that the five distinctions described above are not five different kinds of knowledge nor even levels of knowledge. Knowledge is an intellectual relationship of a person with the world of thought and reality, and is in this person one and undivided. The actual development and actualisation of a person's knowledge may, however, be biased towards one or more of these five aspects of knowledge. This may enhance or impair its quality with regard to insight and understanding and so determine its use or usefulness.

Knowledge which a Primary Teacher should Cultivate

Without going into details of the content of possible maths and science courses in primary teacher training institutions, we can indicate and state that one should strive for as close a balance as one can accomplish between the five outlined emphases, or aspects, of knowledge. In mathematics as well as in science the teachers should become fluent in the appropriate language and use of symbols. They should be rich, and become richer still, in direct experience by a very active and totally involving (workshop) approach. Through reasoning in discussion, reflection on action and thought processes, and wide related reading and discourse, they should gain in comprehension, so that they build up a framework of insightful understanding on which they can rely in their work as well as in their further personal development, with confidence.

Successful teaching of children in mathematics and in science requires a knowledge of the basics, the elements of the subjects. This knowledge requires a deeper understanding than many teachers seem to achieve in their training courses. This seems to indicate and imply that the elements of the primary school's subject matter refers to what lies at the foundation of the sciences, and these foundations are dug deeply. 'Elementary' is therefore by no means to be identified with 'childlike' or 'easy'. These elements, then, are to be pursued in depth in the training courses, rather than superseded by 'more advanced subject matter', whatever that may be.

Apart from having 'necessary' knowledge it is important for the teacher to be aware of having a distinct view of the subject. Is science an accumulation of facts to be conquered by gathering factual knowledge is science itself a way of learning: the operative skill of acquiring knowledge by the intellectual processes of observing, questioning, hypothesising, experimenting and reasoning? An answer to either of these questions will express the teacher's view of science and profoundly influence his mode of teaching the subject. Many people tend to accept that acquiring knowledge of the facts of science is the purpose of science teaching, and would consequently emphasise the orderly organisation of these facts in graded packages for learning, if necessary by rote, but supported by demonstrations and illustrations, according to the assumed intellectual capacity of children in different classes. However, the view of science as an intellectual process of active learning is adhered to by a growing number of educators, and this results in a way of teaching which we could characterise as 'problem posing teaching promoting problem solving learning'.

Similarly, the teaching of mathematics requires some flexibility of approach where mathematical processes enter the picture.For instance, in teaching computation there is more than one way of familiarising the children with algorithms. If teachers tend to teach only 'their own' algorithms, they should become aware that there are many different models, some of which may be invented by the children. The consideration and conscious appreciation of a different algorithm, or indeed any other mathematical model, reaches beyond pure computation and calculation, and helps the children really to understand mathematical processes.

It is insight and intelligence that should be challenged in the future teacher. It should touch upon all the facets of the teacher's knowledge that we have emphasised above. It should not be unduly overbalanced and directed to one particular aspect, as often happens in rote learning.Teacher training courses that move away from the kinds of knowledge that matter leave students bewildered and battered, sighing: This science or this maths is not for me', in which case neither will it be for their children. Teachers need delight and enthusiasm in their own learning, their own formation of knowledge. By being totally immersed and involved in the process of 'making' their own basic knowledge of science and mathematics, they learn to help the children work toward making their own knowledge, too, for there is truth in the remark that teachers tend to teach the way they themselves were taught.

6

Assessment as a Part of Teaching

The view of assessment that we are adopting here is that it is a process in which information is collected about performance, compared with some standard, criterion or expectation and a judgement is made on the extent to which there is a match. In this view, assessment results in a record or response which replaces the actual behaviour. It follows that there is always some selection and some information is lost. Results of assessment are not 'the real thing' and cannot tell the whole story. This must be kept in mind in interpreting and using the results of assessment.

The various ways in which information is collected and the various bases for judging it create the variety of different kinds of assessment. These include standardised tests, where information is gathered whilst children are tackling carefully devised tasks under controlled conditions and, in contrast, ongoing assessment, carried out almost imperceptibly during normal interchange between teacher and pupils.

A major distinction is to be made between tests (and examinations) and other forms of assessment. Tests are specially devised activities designed to assess knowledge and/or skills by giving precisely the same task to pupils who have to respond to it under similar conditions prescribed by those who devised and trialled the test. However the distinction between tests and non-test assessment is not always all that clear. Some 'tests' can be absorbed into classroom work and look very much like normal classroom work as far as the children are concerned and so they cannot always be regarded as 'formal'. Whether formal or informal, of course, tests are only part of assessment.

Pupils are assessed for a number of reasons and the method chosen should suit the purpose. The main groups of purposes are:

— to help teaching (formative assessment)

 To be effective in this role the assessment must be planned, recorded and used.

— to provide a record of achievement (summary) This record is used in ongoing discussion with pupils, in producing a summary of progress and achievements for discussion with parents, and providing information to receiving teachers.

— as a contribution to school effectiveness measures The information here will be about the performance of groups of pupils and should be only one part of the information about the school.

— to provide national performance survey data This may be used to compare performance across various groups of pupils with national targets, to make comparisons from year to year and between sub groups.

In the present context we will confine discussion to the first of these purposes since it is the one which has most impact on the teacher's day to day work.

For pupils to have opportunity for learning with understanding they must have chance to apply the ideas and skills they bring with them to a new experience, and to take part in changing their ideas through using process skills (which are thereby developed). This is the essence of active learning by the child and involves mental and physical activity. The outcome will be ideas which make sense to the child and can be described as being 'owned' by the child.

For there to be the chance of this kind of learning the teacher must find out what are the ideas and skills that children bring to their learning experiences. This is the second step in teaching for understanding, the first being to provide the opportunity for children to engage with materials and problems in an informal way a which will allow their ideas to be elicited. These first and the subsequent steps are represented as follows.

Where work continues on the same topic, the second and fifth steps become the same, both being concerned with ascertaining children's ideas at a particular time. The step of 'providing opportunity for exploration and involvement' ensures that children's thinking is engaged before ideas are sought. When introducing a new topic this initial step will merge into that of 'finding out ideas' where the teacher should be able to choose from a range of assessment methods, including open questioning, asking children to draw and annotate their drawings, encouraging children to write about or talk about their ideas, and at all times listening to what the children have to say.

The 'interpretation' is an important step which may be very short or quite long, depending on the teacher's experience and the nature of the ideas which come from the children. It involves reflecting on the experience which may have lead children to their current ideas and the kinds of reasoning that they are using. It is these things which are the basis for deciding the best way to help children in the next step.

For example, if a child expresses the idea that growth only happens at certain times and is not continuous, the problem may be lack of evidence and the teacher will try to provide new experience which would challenge a view of discontinuous growth. On the other hand, if a child's ideas are highly bound to particular contexts (such as having different explanations for evaporation in different situations) it may not be new evidence which is required, but a discussion of the reasoning, or perhaps the words, being used about evidence already available.

For the step of 'helping children to develop their ideas' the starting point is the ideas which the children have, whether or not these ideas are along the 'right' lines. 'Development' means heightening, extending and strengthening useful ideas as well as challenging ones which are not useful in explaining things.

One of the main ways of doing this involves children in devising and carrying out investigations to test their ideas, but some activities may be less extensive, such as asking children to provide examples of what they mean by certain words they use, encouraging them to apply ideas they use in one context in trying to explain another one, providing a greater range of evidence (including the use of secondary sources) and encouraging reflection and communication. During these activities there are likely to be opportunities for assessment of any change in children's ideas, using the same range of techniques as in the 'finding out' step.

The way in which the steps are described and characterised varies to some extent according to different interpretations of constructivism, but the important common feature is that assessment is embedded in the teaching. It is something that has to be given as much attention in planning as are the materials and the initial activities. Indeed the way in which the materials are used and the nature of the learning experiences will depend on the information gained in the initial assessment.

For example, a teacher planning a lesson on the energy value of different foods started by asking children to look at the information about energy value given on food wrapping and containers. When they began talking about food, the teacher found that many children did not connect food with energy at all. In fact it was sometimes the reverse; they reported feeling sleepy and not at all energetic after a big meal. Their ideas were simply that 'Food keeps us alive. You die if youdon't eat.'

The teacher then modified his plan and led a discussion on the different reasons the children could find for eating. These were gathered from the family at home, from claims made in advertisements, from the school cook. Then they discussed what happened if people did not eat, as well as the reasoning behind the views they had collected. After a few weeks the children had linked food and energy in their minds and so the teacher suggested the investigation of differences in this respect since this had become a real issue for the children.

Assessing Active Learning

For assessment to have a role in teaching it must comprehensively encompass all learning aims, whether of skill, concept or attitude development. This and other points made so far apply to all subjects, but there arise some particular problems shared by mathematics and science. Active learning, where mental and physical skills are being developed, and where how things are done is as important as what things are done, poses a challenge for assessment.

Whilst much can be done through study of the products of children's work, it is also important to obtain information about, for example in a mathematics problem, how results were arrived at, whether the appropriate mathematical model was used, how operations were planned, what checks were carried out. In science the equivalent matters include whether tests carried out were 'fair', whether necessary variables were controlled, whether all evidence was taken into account and valid conclusions drawn from it.

Experienced teachers pick up this information during their normal interaction with children as part of teaching, but it poses considerable problems for novice teachers or for those who are introducing active approaches to learning in their classrooms for the first time. These teachers need help to use assessment in the pursuit of active learning, for which conventional methods of assessment are inadequate.

The help teachers need in relation to assessing active learning includes guidance in these three matters:

- what to assess
- how to collect information systematically
- how to involve children in the process.

What To Assess

Assessing children during active learning is not just a matter of seeing whether or not they are observing, hypothesising, selecting appropriate models, checking, etc. Such broad judgements would have little value for helping the children's learning and in any case could not be made without first thinking through what it means to observe, hypothesise and so on. A first step, therefore, is to have some general indicators of what children are doing when carrying out the processes. The form these might take is best suggested through an example. At a workshop for teacher educators, the following indicators were among those identified for process skills:

Obsewing

- using the senses (as many as safe and appropriate) to gather information
- identifying differences between similar objects or events
- identifying similarities between different objects or events
- noticing fine details that are relevant to an investigation
- recognising the order in which sequenced events take place
- looking for patterns that may exist in observations, etc.

Finding patterns and relationships

- putting various pieces of information (from direct observation or secondary sources) together and inferring something from them
- using patterns or relationships in information, measurements or observations to make predictions

- identifying trends or relationships in information
- realising the difference between a conclusion that fits all the evidence and an interference that goes beyond it etc.

Hypothesising

- attempting to explain observations or relationships in terms of some principle or concept applying concepts or knowledge gained in one situation to help understanding, or to solve a problem in another
- recognising that there can be more than one possible explanation of an event
- realising the need to test explanations by gathering more evidence, etc.

Raising questions

- asking questions which lead to enquiry
- asking questions for information
- asking questions based on hypotheses
- realising that they can find out answers to some of their questions by their own investigation
- putting questions into a testable form
- recognising that some questions cannot be answered by enquiry etc.

Devising investigations

- deciding what equipment, materials, etc are needed for an investigations

- identifying what is to change or be changed when different observations or measurements are made
- identifying what variables are to be kept the same for a fair test
- identifying what is to be measured or compared
- considering beforehand how the measurements,

  comparisons etc, are to be used to solve the problem
- deciding the order in which steps should be taken in the investigation etc

Respect for evidence

- reporting what actually happens even if this is in conflict with expectations
- querying and checking parts of the evidence which do not fit into the pattern of other findings
- querying a conclusion or interpretation for which there is insufficient evidence
- treating ideas or conclusions as provisional and as being open to challenge by further evidence

Critical reflection

- willingness to review what they have done in order to consider how it might have been improved
- considering alternative procedures to those used
- identifying the points in favour and against the way in which an investigation was carried out or its results interpreted
- using critical reflection of a previous investigation in planning and carrying out a later one

A valuable workshop activity is for groups of teachers to work out these indicators for themselves. In doing so they will be clarifying the meaning of the process skills and attitudes and acquiring some ownership over the common definitions to be used. The indicators have to become part of the mental framework the teacher carries in his/her head, used in gathering information through watching children, listening to them, discussing with them what they are doing, as well as from any products in the form of writing, drawings or artefacts.

In use the general indicators have to be translated into the context of specific activities. What will children be doing or saying as evidence of the skills and attitudes when they are investigating vegetation along a transect, working out prime numbers, finding the relationship between masses on a balance—or investigating the melting of ice? A class of 7 and 8 year olds was entranced by a very large block of ice floating in water 141. In their interaction, discussion and related investigations they showed evidence of

Observing

— they pointed out details of 'lines' and air bubbles in the ice and places where it was opaque

— they used their sense of touch to feel the 'stickiness' of the ice when just out of the freezer

— they noticed the sequence in which parts of the block started melting.

Finding patterns and relationships

— they linked together pieces of information in finding that the larger pieces which they broke off slid down a slope more easily than smaller pieces

- they found a pattern relating the size of pieces of ice to how quickly they melted
- they noted that the parts of the block in the water were melting first but showed caution in saying that 'it isn't everything that will melt more quickly in water than in air'.
- they reported evidence contrary to their ideas: 'moisture still forms on the outside of the tank when there is a cover on it, but I thought it wouldn't' 1 querying whether there is air in the bubbles in the ice: 'we don't know the bubbles are air, we think they are'.

Critical reflection

- criticising their investigation of the effect of size on rate of melting: 'it would have been better to start with some larger pieces, then the difference would have shown up more'
- criticising a comparison of melting in and out of water: 'we should have held the piece in air above the table so that they weren't sitting in the water when they melted'.

Again, practice in 'translating' general indicators into evidence in the context of particular activities can be usefully carried out in teachers' workshops, where added value comes from considering the potential for learning in various activities. The importance of maintaining rigour in the assessment has to be emphasised; the indicators are the criteria against which the children's performance is assessed. Whilst the particular ways in which the skills and attitudes are made evident vary infinitely in various activities, it must be possible to show that they are all variants of the behaviours described by the general criteria.

Systematic Assessing

Teachers new to the idea of assessing children during their activities can be overwhelmed by the scale of the task. How can all the children be observed all the time? They can't be, of course. What is required is for the teacher to plan to observe and make notes about one particular group during an investigation, which could spread over several sessions. The teacher would not be standing and watching this group for long periods; indeed the special focus in his/her mind should not be apparent to the children.

The difference should be in the identification of particular kinds of information which the teacher is gathering during interaction with the group and in the notes (mental and perhaps written) made at the time about each child in the group. This is not in practice as demanding as it may at first seem, as the example of the ice block activities may have indicated.

In a subsequent investigation another group of pupils would be the targets' of observation and so on until all the members of the class have been assessed. A benefit of planning the assessment in this way is that information is gathered about all children, not just the ones who claim most of the teacher's attention.

A consequence of this approach, however, that pupils will be assessed on the same skills but when engaged upon different activities. The question as to whether this matters takes us back the point about careful application of criteria. It is a useful focus for discussion in a workshop, as is the development of skill in assessing individual pupils working within a group. Ideally teachers or students should try out suggestions in classes in between workshop sessions.

INVOLVING CHILDREN IN ASSESSMENT

Involving children in assessment has several benefits. It can ease the teachers burden of assessment, but perhaps more importantly enables the children to take a positive role in their learning. But it means that children must know what are the aims of their learning. Communicating these aims not easy since directly telling about complex learning objectives and criteria of achievement is unlikely to be successful. So self-assessment skill has to be developed slowly and in an accepting and supportive atmosphere takes time to work through several stages before children are able to apply to their achievement anything like the criteria which their teacher would apply.

The process can begin usefully if children from about the age of eight are encouraged to select their 'best' work and to put this in a folder or bag. Part of the time for 'bagging' should be set aside for the teacher to talk to each child about why certain pieces of work were selected. The criteria which the children are using will become clear. Whatever they are, they should be accepted; they may have messages for the teacher.

For example if work seems to be selected only on the basis of being 'tidy' and not in terms of content, then perhaps this aspect is being over emphasised. At first the discussion should only be to clarify the criteria the children use. 'Tell me what you particularly liked about this piece of work? Gradually it will be possible to suggest criteria without dictating what the children should be selecting. Through such an approach as this children may begin to share the understanding of the objectives of their work and will be able to comment usefully on what they have learned. It then becomes easier to be explicit about further targets and for the children to recognise when they have achieved them. This is part of building confidence in pupils that their part in assessment is valued and that it can make their learning more enjoyable.

Using a somewhat similar approach to teachers in training has the same value for them as learners. Regularly they should be asked to comment on what part of their course they enjoy most—and least—and why. They should also be asked to identify what they have learned, as distinct from what they have done, and to reflect on the circumstances which affected their learning. They will then realise, from their own experience, the value of being asked to assess their own work and may then be more likely to give their pupils this opportunity.

7

Training Needs of Teachers

All the aims of teacher training cannot be achieved in an initial course. Therefore, it may be helpful to distinguish between what should be provided in pre-service courses and what could or should be provided through in-service courses. In attempting to draw this line there will inevitably be contention about what is essential as a 'basic minimum' for the beginning teacher and the matter will generally be decided in specific cases by the constraints of time and the consideration of the context of the training.

Time is necessarily limited in initial teacher education courses, especially where, as is usually the case in primary education, the teachers are being prepared to teach all subjects right across the curriculum. The timing and structure of pre-service courses also limits what can be achieved for the development of certain attributes of effective teaching requires experience of a sustained relationship with children and colleagues, and perhaps also with pupils' parents, which is generally not available at the initial stage. Therefore, where these attributes are not essential for the beginning teacher, their development need not be an aim of an initial course designed for the regular classroom teacher. In this argument, however, there is an assumption about the provision of opportunities for continued professional development which should be available.

The pace of change in teaching and the need to maintain the relevance of curriculum to children's everyday lives mean that in-service education is essential for other reasons than complementing pre-service education. However, if it is not available as an entitlement, then more than the base line minimum has to be included in the initial course. What is possible in this respect varies with course structures. For example, courses where students spend a large portion of the time in schools will differ from those which are mainly institution based. With these points in mind, then, we propose the following lists for discussion.

Proposals for core opportunities to be provided in initial teacher education courses:

- experience of the nature of scientific and mathematical activity
- experiences which generate an enthusiasm for science and mathematics
- activities which supplement personal knowledge and understanding of the subjects to a level beyond that expected of the children they are to teach
- experiences which inculcate the scientific attitudes of willingness to tolerate uncertainty, respect for evidence and open mindedness, and the professional attitudes of empathy, willingness to take responsibility and integrity
- activities which develop personal understanding of science processes and mathematical thinking

- studying the development of scientific and mathematical understanding and relating it to learning in general
- studying and practising assessment of pupils during regular work and through structured tasks
- using the information so gained to match activities to pupils' progress
- planning the content and organisation of science and mathematics activities for children within a given school programme
- observing, evaluating and practising strategies for-classroom control, with particular reference to practical science and mathematics activities
- studying a range of teaching styles and practising some of them
- acquiring familiarity with the required syllabus and with available published resources
- identifying and using criteria for selecting and adapting available classroom material l experience of selecting and improvising simple equipment
- experiences designed to develop skill in handling and using productively children's questions l studying and practising ways of encouraging children's communication and recording for various purposes and audiences
- making use of information technology in science and mathematics activities
- experience of techniques for, and encouragement of the habit of, self-appraisal

- study of where and how science and mathematics can usefully be combined in integrated or cross-curricular topics and approaches
- recognising and avoiding sources of bias or inequality of opportunity relating to gender, ethnicity, and physical handicap.

Additional Opportunities Which May Be Provided Through In-Service Programmes

The needs of teachers for continued professional development and the extension of responsibility beyond their classroom requires opportunities for

- further development of all skills, attitudes, knowledge and

  understanding indicated in the above items
- studying ways of catering for children with special needs
- experiencing programme planning at the whole school level
- developing skills of working with colleagues and of liaison

  with other schools, both primary and secondary
- interpreting and using records and results of assessment
- reporting to parents and to school board members (if appropriate)
- communicating to parents and the local community the

  objectives of the school and dealing with queries

- selection and organisation of equipment and resources
- continued development of the use of information technology in teaching and learning science and mathematics. .
- developing classroom research skills
- incorporating science and mathematics experiences into the curriculum of preschool children.

Learning of Teacher Trainees

Trainee teachers' ideas of teaching are likely to have to be changed, but changed in a way which gives them ownership of the new ideas. This means that the ideas make sense in terms of experience and reasoning, both of which have to be provided in the training course. Thus the course must give them the opportunities for realising the nature and the value of the kind of learning which leads to ownership through themselves learning in this way.

So, for example, when learning about the nature of scientific and mathematical activity, they should be working in the same way and it is intended that they work with children; being active physically and mentally. There should be some time in which they can undertake simple scientific investigations and mathematical tasks in a way which creates the excitement and enthusiasm of finding solutions through their own activity. After experiences of this kind, however, as adults and teachers, they can stand back and consider what they have been doing and examine their learning. They will then be able to think out for themselves how to make these sorts of experiences available to children. Then their previous assumptions about teaching will be challenged and their ideas changed.

This way of learning in teacher education does not have to be restricted to developing personal knowledge of science and mathematics and considering appropriate activities for children. It can and should be applied in all the experiences listed above. It means using the ideas which are already present in the trainees as the starting point, whether these are about how to answer children's questions, about how to assess children's understanding, about class organisation or about using equipment. In all these cases active learning can be implemented, producing an atmosphere where evidence and logical reasoning is used and everyone's ideas are respected and openly discussed.

A further advantage of this approach is that it fosters positive attitudes such as respect for evidence, open mindedness, tolerance and willingness to review actions and arguments critically. Recalling that attitudes are caught not taught, however, means that this has implications for the training of teacher educators.

Integration of Maths & Science In Teacher Education Courses

The fact that a single list of opportunities covering both science and mathematics has been proposed here, suggests that there are many similarities in what is required by primary teachers in relation to these subjects. The possibility of time-conserving cooperation appears to be present, but nevertheless it would be perfectly logical to run two separate courses, with one providing the opportunities in relation to mathematics and the other having the same function for science.

Course structure often determines the extent to which the teaching of science and mathematics can be studied together or in cross-curricular topics. Many courses begin from study of separately identified subjects so that these can be recognised in integrated topics which are introduced later; others begin in a more holistic way which requires considerable collaborative planning on the part of those involved in a primary teacher education course. Since national or local curriculum guidelines usually exist as subject based documents, if integration is desired then it is important for teacher education to avoid further reinforcing the subject divisions through its course structures.

This joint planning and shared sessions in many areas of professional development would not only assist in the 'litre into the half-litre pot' problem, but would be the best means of educating primary teachers—as opposed to teachers who change personae from 'science teacher' to 'maths teacher, from one part of the day to the next. The way in which the teacher education course is organised may well have to strike a balance between what the logic of the two subjects dictates and what is expected in the schools (which does not always follow this logic). Teachers will need not only to consider but to experience some integrated work in their initial training if they are to practise it with understanding.

TEACHER EDUCATION APPROACHES

The Concept of Activity

The history of learning theory shows an increasing attention to learners' activities. Olsen, a Norwegian mathematics teacher educator, uses the word 'Activity' with a capital A to stress that real learning takes place when situation, problem and activities have a 'political value for the students. What they do must be of importance to their own lives, they must experience an improvement of circumstances because of their learning activity. The concept of 'ownership' has similar import. This is what student teachers should experience in their courses; activities which are important to their professional lives, as teachers-to-be now and eventually as teachers in their own classrooms. Close to the concept of activity are 'interaction', 'reflection' and production'. Working together in small cooperative groups stimulates those actions in which intuitive notions, beliefs, former experiences, pre conceptions and informal procedures can be brought in, discussed and accommodated. Meanings are developed and shared as participants put their ideas into words to explain them to others. To do this, reflection thinking about your own activity, even about your own thinking appears to be necessary.

Teacher educators, who teach this view of learning in their courses, cannot neglect it in designing their own teacher education. This means that in the courses there must be room for cooperative work in which attention is paid to the students' subjective theories, their own learning-histories, their beliefs and conceptions with regard to the school-subjects they study, and their philosophy of the disciplines behind these subjects.

It also means that teacher education courses must provide room for production, reflection and interaction in situations, and with problems to solve which future teachers recognise as real problems and which strongly motivate them. Sometimes conflicts arise, for instance, when personal theories do not fit into new ideas about learning and teaching. In this case the teacher educator is challenged to create a learning environment for students in which interaction, reflection and their own ideas set the course.

Dimensions of Activity in Teacher Education

Many primary teacher students have received from their own education a legacy of failure, or at least dissatisfaction, in relation to mathematics and science. Therefore, their first and foremost requirement is to acquire confidence, to gain an appreciation of the nature of scientific and mathematical activity, and to development husiasm for teaching mathematics and science. The educator of teachers who is guided by this idea creates opportunities for participation and investigation by the students and thinks in terms of learning environments'.

Students must be active in the learning environment, in relation to the (school) subject matter, to the pedagogy of the subject and to what is going on in classrooms when this subject is being taught. Within this we can identify three dimensions of activity in teacher education:

- studying the (school) subject means that the student teachers own knowledge and ability is brought up to the required level. If possible the studies extend around the subjects so that further relationships and deeper insight into the discipline emerge. Sometimes the history of science and mathematics can contribute, particularly when developments in the past give cues for learning in classrooms now. Mastery of the subject for teachers does not mean advanced study beyond the basics.
- developmental work and research in both domains contributes to the body of pedagogical knowledge. This knowledge becomes the subject of activity in teacher education. There, as the (school) subject comes to life closer to classroom practice, students are further stimulated to improve their own standards of knowledge, but now from the perspective of being a teacher.
- classroom practice is viewed as an experimental field in which learning and teaching can be investigated, designed and practised.

If we compare science and mathematics in the framework of these dimensions, similarities and differences emerge. For example, with respect to the first dimension, in primary mathematics the teacher's own skill in calculation plays a more important role than in science. It is that instrumental character of mathematics Bishop speaks of 'symbolic technology' that makes a difference in the pedagogical dimension as well. Student teachers often have to work hard to acquire the basic skills of mathematics, which they should have memorised during their own years of primary school, but often did not do. In science there is less need for memorised factual knowledge.

In both subjects a large amount of psychological research has taken place from which many contributions to pedagogical knowledge have come. Together with the results of developmental projects, this means that a considerable amount of knowledge is available with regard to both subjects. Science and mathematics are also very close in the third dimension. Learning to teach in the classrooms requires a study of learning processes, knowing how to start those processes and how to support and supervise them and what materials can be used.

Teaching Workshops

A workshop is a direct way of providing a learning experience in which the learner creates meaning or understanding through his or her mental or physical activity. What is provided as a basis for this action can be objects or materials to investigate or use, or problems to solve, or evidence to examine and discuss, or all these together. The outcome may be an artefact, a solution to a problem, a plan, there cognition of a new relationship between things, a critique or a set of criteria. Perhaps the most important product, however, is a greater understanding of how to achieve such results.

Workshops of this kind have been well developed in science. Not only is the scientific phenomenon at hand the subject of investigation, but so are the investigators and the investigation itself. All those involved stand back from their involvement and reflect on their role, their interaction with each other and with the materials and consider the role of the materials used and the educational setting. These workshops in science have the three characteristics of the learning environment for student teachers, mentioned earlier. They can also provide opportunities for the activities.

This kind of workshop is in many respects quite similar to what in mathematics is called a 'mathematical-didactical' workshop. Student teachers cooperatively and thus inter actively solve mathematical problems at their own level, similar to the way children would do it at their levels. All the three dimensions are taken care of, so that not only the mathematical subject matter, but the pedagogical knowledge and the learning and teaching of this subject matter become issues of study as well. A few examples illustrate specific workshops, for

- mathematical problem solving
- explaining mathematics
- analysing concrete materials for use in primary schools
- educational design
- creating help for low achievers.

The educator of primary mathematics teachers must pay particular attention to issues like:

- studying children's strategies in acquiring number concepts and the way school books teach it
- observing children's learning of algorithms and the way school books teach it.

Investigating The Differences

'Learning to teach science' and 'learning to teach mathematics' are to be distinguished. There are essential differences in the nature of knowledge in the subjects. The following will illustrate this point of view. Take the activity of 'organising', which in both, science as well as in mathematics, is considered as basic and fundamental. But, as we shall see, it has in each subject a very different interpretation and application.

In the science workshop organising (the investigation) means to gather data systematically in order to get knowledge about the object of the current investigation, to be able to make a clear description of the phenomenon, to create possibilities for investigating details, to ask better questions, to manage the answers in order to check earlier hypotheses etc. Organising in science workshops serves the investigation.

Organising in mathematics not only facilitates the problem solving activity, but it also affects the way in which the knowledge is organised in children's minds. A specific organisation of 'situations of division' leads to a specific algorithm constructed in the children's minds. Using a city plan to organise multiplication-situations affects the way a related thinking model (in this case the grid model) arises in the minds of the pupils. This means that in mathematics organising structures the knowledge itself and, because such knowledge could be strongly context-bound, it is necessary to investigate other contexts with a similar structure (isomorphic problems) that permit the same organisation. From a broader point of view all kinds of organisation can be seen as part of 'mathematising'. In all particular situations mathematising stands for organisation, discovering a structure, creating a useful notation schema, inventing short-cuts. All these activities affect the structure of developing personal knowledge.

Commonalities

In the foregoing paragraphs a number of similarities between primary science and mathematics passed in review. Summarising we conclude that learning to teach both subjects in primary school

- demands opportunities for student teachers to overcome dissatisfaction from the past and to create new perspectives on the subjects
- needs activity with interactive, reflective and productive participation in investigation.
- has to take into account students' own ideas and personal, subjective theories
- must pay much attention to children's learning processes in science and mathematics
- is organised in a 'reflective model' of teacher education.

Balancing the differences and similarities it becomes possible to draw some conclusions. When designing teacher education it must be possible to realise collaboration between science and mathematics, but recommending total integration of both domains in teacher education, would be unwise. The identified differences ask for a clear distinction, the existence of fundamental commonalities suggest a carefully thought-out 'mixed economy', certainly not only to save learning time, but because a mixed economy of science and mathematics teaching in the colleges of education really can be richer than teaching the subject areas separately. A mixed economy in teacher education for instance means combined science and mathematical pedagogic workshops, with maths activities in a science context, as starting points for a study of learning and design practice.

This mixed economy may be the best from the teachers' point of view. If the differences are clear and the teacher has enough self-confidence to teach both subjects 'actively', it will be worthwhile sometimes to use mathematics in order to deepen science understanding or to use a science context to develop a mathematical skill. Between the separated approach and the advanced integration of the two, many variants are possible. At the secondary school level one subject is used as a field of practice for the other.

At the primary level the similarities in pedagogy weighs more heavily than the need to reflect the distinctions between the disciplines. These differences should be considered by both teacher educators and trainee teachers in relation to their own teaching. The role of teacher education is to provide the knowledge and awareness which will support a greater proportion of integrated work. If students and teachers encounter mathematics and science only in separate compartments, their ability to combine the two is unlikely to grow. Some of their work should be clearly focused on each subject so that the identity of mathematical and scientific activity can be in no doubt, but some should be integrated so that points of contact can increasingly be recognised.

8

Phonological Training

Phonemic understanding is essential to learning to read an alphabetic language. The majority of children with reading disabilities fail to grasp this idea.

- In teaching phonemic awareness, the focus of all activities should be on the sounds of words, not on letters or spellings.
- Use strategies that make phonemes prominent in children's attention and perception. For example, model specific sounds, such as /s/ in the word sat, and ask children to produce each sound in isolation and in many different words until they are comfortable with the sound and understand its nature.
- Begin with simple words and simple challenges, e.g., listen for initial /s/ in sat, sit, sip, and sad or for long /e/ in me, see, bee . .
- Teach students to blend phonemes into words. Begin by identifying just one phoneme, e.g., /m/-ilk, /s/-at, working gradually toward blending all the phonemes in words, e.g., /s/-/a/-/t/.
- Teach students to identify the separate phonemes within words, e.g., what is the first sound of soup?

What is the last sound of kiss? Beginning phonemes are easier to identify than final phonemes.

- Once students are comfortable listening for individual phonemes, teach them to break up words, into component sounds, e.g., /m/-/oo/-/s/= "moose".
- Create a sequence of segmenting and blending activities to help students develop an understanding of the relationship between sounds in words.
- Provide children with more support when first teaching a task. For example, model a sound or strategy for making the sound, and have the children use the strategy to produce the sound. Model and practice several examples. Prompt the children to use the strategy during guided practice, and gradually add more examples. As the students master these skills, provide less teacher-directed instruction and more practice and challenge.
- Make teaching phonological awareness a top priority. Opportunities to engage in phonological awareness activities should be plentiful, frequent, brief, and fun.
- Phonemic awareness is essential for learning to read, but it is not enough by itself. It must be coupled with instruction and practice in learning the relationship between letters and sounds.

Sounds and Letters

- Students should learn the letters of the alphabet and discriminate each letter from the other, because each stands for one or more of the sounds that occur in spoken words.

- When presenting each letter, model its corresponding sound and have children produce the sound themselves. For children with learning disabilities, the teaching activities must be explicit and unambiguous.
- At first, teach and work with only a few letter-sound correspondences that have high utility in many words (e.g., /m/ in man, mad, him, and ham). Postpone teaching less frequently occurring letters until students have a firm understanding of how left-to-right spellings represent first-to-last sounds.
- After students have mastered a few letter-sound correspondences, teach them to decode words or sound them out. Begin with small, familiar words. Teach the children to sound out the letters, left to right, and blend them together, searching for the word in memory.
- Model sounding out the word, blending the sounds together and saying the word. The ability to sound out new words allows children to identify and learn new words on their own.
- Give children stories containing words that reflect the letter-sound patterns that have been taught, and encourage them to sound out words whenever they are uncertain.
- Help children learn spelling conventions, such as the use of final /e/'s to mark long vowels, by comparing and contrasting lots of examples.

Spell Words

- Teach children to spell words by sounding their letters one by one. Model the sounding and spelling process for children as they spell.

- Begin with short words children can sound out, because these words follow regular spelling conventions, e.g., cap, bat, and sit instead of cape, bait or sight.
- Begin with simple words that do not contain consonant blends, e.g., ham and pan instead of slam and plan.
- Encourage students to use spelling knowledge and strategies regularly in their own writing.
- Introduce spelling conventions systematically. Begin with words that exemplify the most frequent and basic conventions, and provide support and practice to help students generalize from these words to others. The goal is to help them see the spelling conventions in the words.
- Use words in which letter-sound correspondences represent their most common sounds.
- Develop a sequence and schedule of opportunities that allow children to apply and develop facility with sounds and words at their own pace. Specify what skills to assess and when to assess them so that you will know when to move on. Take into account each student's background knowledge and pace in moving from sounding out to blending words to reading connected text.

Reflective Reading

- Help children learn to read fluently by requiring them to read new stories and reread old stories every day.
- Help children extend their experience with the words, language, and ideas in books by interactively reading harder texts with them and to them every day.

– Relate information in books to other events of interest to children, such as holidays, pets, siblings, and games. Engage children in discussion of the topics.

– In both stories and informational texts, encourage wondering. For example, "I wonder what Pooh will do now?" "How do you think the father feels ?" or "I wonder what frogs do in the winter? Do you think that's a problem? Why?"

– Model comprehension strategies and provide students with guided assistance.

One of the most compelling findings from recent reading research is that children who get off to a poor start in reading rarely catch up. As several studies have now documented, the poor first-grade reader almost invariably continues to be a poor reader. And the consequences of a slow start in reading become monumental as they accumulate exponentially over time. The best solution to the problem of reading failure is to allocate resources for early identification and prevention. It is a tragedy of the first order that while we know clearly the costs of waiting too long, few school districts have in place a mechanism to identify and help children before failure takes hold. Indeed, in the majority of cases, there is no systematic identification until third grade, by which time successful remediation is more difficult and more costly.

School-based preventive efforts should be engineered to maintain growth in critical word reading skills at roughly normal levels throughout the early elementary school period. Although adequate development of these skills in first grade does not guarantee that children will continue to maintain normal growth in second grade without extra help, to the extent that we allow children to fall seriously behind at any point during early elementary school, we are moving to a "remedial" rather than a "preventive" model of intervention.

Once children fall behind in the growth of critical word reading skills, it may require very intensive interventions to bring them back up to adequate levels of reading accuracy, and reading fluency may be even more difficult to restore because of the large amount of reading practice that is lost by children each month and year that they remain poor readers.

The first of these "assumptions" is, in fact, a self-evident value judgment. Adequate reading comprehension is the most important ultimate outcome of effective instruction in reading. The ultimate purpose of reading instruction is to help children acquire the skills that enable learning from, understanding, and enjoyment of written language. This "assumption" is not controversial. No matter what one's personal preferences for instructional method, the end goal is to help children comprehend written material at a level that is consistent with their general intellectual abilities. Two general types of skill and knowledge are required for good reading comprehension. Consistent with Gough's "simple view of reading", comprehension of written material requires: 1) general language comprehension ability; and 2) ability to accurately and fluently identify the words in print.

Knowledge and active application of specific reading strategies is also required to maximize reading comprehension but most of the variability among children and adults in comprehension of written material can be accounted for by measuring the two broad families of skills identified in Gough's simple view. That is, good general language comprehension and good word reading skills are the most critical skills required for effective comprehension of written material.

Most children who become poor readers experience early and continuing difficulties in learning how to accurately identify printed words. This difficulty is expressed most directly on two kinds of reading tasks. First, children destined to be poor readers at the end of elementary school almost invariably have difficulties understanding and applying the alphabetic principle in deciphering unfamiliar words. These children have unusual difficulties learning to use the regular patterns of correspondence between letters and sounds in words as an aid in identifying new words they encounter in text. They have trouble "sounding out" unknown words. Second, poor readers at all grade levels are characterized by slower than normal development of a "sight vocabulary" of words they can read fluently and automatically. Ultimately, it is this difficulty in rapid word recognition that limits comprehension in older poor readers, for these skills allow children to focus on constructing the meaning of what they are reading rather than spending too many of their intellectual resources on trying to identify the words. The strongest current theories of reading growth link phonetic and "sight word" reading skills together by showing how good phonetic reading skills are necessary in the formation of accurate memory for the spelling patterns that are the basis of sight word recognition. The most common cause of difficulties acquiring early word reading skills is weakness in the ability to process the phonological features of language.

This is perhaps the most important discovery about reading difficulties in the last twenty years. Weaknesses in the phonological area of language development can be measured by a variety of nonreading tasks, but the ones most commonly used assess phonemic awareness, which can be defined simply as the ability to identify, think about, or manipulate the individual sounds in words. Much of our new confidence in being able to identify children at risk for reading failure before reading instruction begins depends on the use of tests of phonemic awareness, since this ability has been shown to be causally related to the growth of early word reading skills. Discovery of the core phonological problems associated with specific reading disability has had at least one unanticipated consequence. The ability to assess these core language problems directly has led to the discovery that the early word reading difficulties of children with relatively low general intelligence and verbal ability are associated with the same factors (weaknesses in phonological processing) that interfere with early reading growth in children who have general intelligence in the normal range. So, weaknesses in phonemic awareness characterize children with reading problems across a broad span of general verbal ability.

On the one hand, many children enter school with adequate general verbal ability and cognitive weaknesses limited to the phonological/language domain. Their primary problem in learning to read involves learning to translate between printed and oral language. On the other hand, another significant group of poor readers, composed largely of children from families of lower socio-economic or minority status, enter school significantly delayed in a much broader range of prereading skills. Since these children are delayed not only in phonological but also in general oral language skills, they are deficient in both of the critical kinds of knowledge and skill required for good reading comprehension. Even if these children can acquire adequate word reading skill, their ability to comprehend the meaning of what they read may be limited by their weak general verbal abilities. Children with general oral language weaknesses require extra instruction in a broader range of knowledge and skills than those who come to school impaired only in phonological ability. What is well established at this point, though, is that both kinds of children will require special support in the growth of early word reading skills if they are to make adequate progress in learning to read.

Quality of Instruction

It is beyond the scope of instructional methods for children with phonological processing weaknesses in any depth at all. In broad stroke, they will benefit from the same approach to reading instruction as children with normal abilities in this area - structured, systematic, and explicit - but for this at-risk group, such instruction is not just beneficial, it is critical. As experienced teachers understand, we cannot assume that these children will acquire any necessary skill for reading words unless they are directly taught that skill or knowledge and receive sufficient opportunities to practice it.

Some of the word-level skills and knowledge these children will require instruction on include: phonemic awareness, letter-sound correspondences, blending skills, a small number of pronunciation conventions (i.e., silent e rule), use of context to help specify a word once it is partially or completely phonemically decoded, strategies for multi-syllable words, and automatic recognition of high-frequency "irregular" words. It goes almost without saying that this type of instruction should be embedded within as many opportunities for meaningful reading and writing as possible.

The lesson from recent large-scale prevention studies is that it is possible to maintain critical word reading skills of most children at risk for reading failure at roughly average levels if this type of instruction is provided beginning sometime during kindergarten or first grade. However, it is also true that in all studies conducted to date, substantial proportions of children with the most severe weaknesses remain significantly impaired in these critical skills following intervention. For example, if we adopt the 30th percentile as a standard for adequate reading progress, then the proportion of the total population remaining at risk in spite of the best interventions tested to date ranges from 5 percent to 7 percent.

Although these results are clearly better than the 30 percent to 60 percent of children who frequently fall below these standards without special interventions, they nevertheless suggest that there is a core of disabled readers in the population for whom we have not yet solved the reading puzzle.Greater intensity and duration of instruction is required because the increased explicitness of instruction for children who are at risk for reading failure requires that more things be taught directly by the teacher. Intensity of instruction is increased primarily by reducing teacher/student ratios. Unless beginning reading instruction for children with phonological weaknesses is more intensive (or lasts significantly longer) than normal instruction, these children will necessarily lag significantly behind their peers in reading growth. An effective preventive program may involve several levels of instructional intensity ranging from small-group to one-on-one instruction, depending upon the severity of the risk factors for each child.

These factors are considered together because they are both tied directly to the availability of accurate identification procedures at various age levels. That is, to be most efficient, a preventive program should be focused on the children who are most in need of special instruction. The efficiency of the entire process will be improved if procedures are available to accurately target the right children very early in the process of reading instruction. Although timing issues with regard to preventive instruction have not been completely resolved by research,we do know, for example, that instruction in phonological awareness during kindergarten can have a positive effect on reading growth after formal reading instruction begins in the first grade.The assumption that it will be useful to identify high-risk children at some time during the kindergarten year so that preventive work may begin as early as possible.

Suggestions Reading

The primary purpose of this section is to make some practical suggestions about procedures and tests that can be used to identify children for preventive reading or prereading instruction. From the outset, however, it is important to recognize that our ability to predict which children will have the most serious reading difficulties is still far from perfect. For example, in a recent comprehensive review of early identification research, Scarborough pointed out that all studies continue to report substantial levels of two kinds of prediction errors. False positive errors are made when children who will eventually become good readers score below the cut-off score on the predictive instrument and are falsely identified as "at risk."

In general, the proportion of this type of error has ranged between 20 percent and 60 percent, with an average of around 45 percent. That is, almost half of the children identified during kindergarten as "at risk" turn out not to have serious reading problems by the end of first grade. False negative errors occur when children who later exhibit reading problems are identified as not being at risk. Typical percentages of false negative errors range from 10 percent to 50 percent, with an average of around 22 percent. That is, on average, current procedures failed to identify about 22 percent of children who eventually end up with serious reading difficulties.

In any given study, the relative proportion of false positive and false negative errors is somewhat arbitrary, since it depends on the level of the cut-off score. For example, we reported a significant reduction in the percentage of false negative errors within the same sample of children by doubling the number of children we identified as at risk. The goal was to identify, during the first semester of kindergarten, the children most at risk to be in the bottom 10 percent in word reading ability by the beginning of second grade. When we selected the 10 percent of children who scored lowest on our predictive tests, our false negative rate was 42 percent.

However, when we identified the 20 percent of children who scored lowest on our measures, the false negative rate was reduced to 8 percent. As a practical matter, if schools desire to maximize their chances for early intervention with the most impaired children, they should provide this intervention to as many children as possible.This is less of a waste of resources than it might seem at first glance, because, although many of the falsely identified children receiving intervention may not be among the most seriously disabled readers, most of them are likely to be below-average readers. Two other pieces of information are relevant to the selection of procedures for early identification of children at risk for reading difficulties. First, prediction accuracy increases significantly the longer a child has been in school. Prediction of reading disabilities from tests given at the beginning of first grade is significantly more accurate than from tests administered during the first semester of kindergarten. Given the widely varying range of children's preschool learning opportunities, many children may score low on early identification instruments in the first semester of kindergarten simply because they have not had the opportunity to learn the skills. Second, although batteries containing multiple tests generally provide better prediction than single instruments, the increase in efficiency of multi-test batteries is generally not large enough to warrant the extra time and resources required to administer them. Thus, we can recommend an identification procedure involving administration of two tests: 1) a test of knowledge of letter names or sounds; and 2) a measure of phonemic awareness. Measures of letter knowledge continue to be the best single predictor of reading difficulties, and measures of phonemic awareness contribute additional predictive accuracy.

In this experience, tests of letter name knowledge are most predictive for kindergarten children, and tests of letter-sound knowledge are most predictive for first graders. Since reading growth is influenced by noncognitive factors such as attention/motivation and home background, as well as specific knowledge and skills, scores from these objective tests might profitably be supplemented with teacher ratings of behavior and attention to identify children most at risk for subsequent difficulties in learning to read.

Since researchers first began to study phonological awareness in the early 1970s, more than twenty different tasks have been used to measure awareness of phonemes in words. These measures can be grouped into three broad categories: sound comparison, phoneme segmentation, and phoneme blending.

Sound comparison tasks use a number of different formats that all require children to make comparisons between the sounds in different words. For example, a child might be asked to indicate which word (of several) begins or ends with the same sound as a target word (i.e., "Which word begins with the same first sound as cat: boy, cake, or fan?"). Additionally, tasks that require children to generate words that have the same first or last sound as a target word would fall in this category. Sound comparison tasks are among the least difficult measures of phonemic awareness, and thus are particularly appropriate for kindergarten age children. *Phoneme segmentation tasks* involve counting, pronouncing, deleting, adding, or reversing the individual phonemes in words. Common examples of this type of task require pronouncing the individual phonemes in words ("Say the sounds in cat one at a time.'), deleting sounds from words ("Say card without saying the /d/ sound."), or counting sounds ("Put one marker on the line for each sound you hear in the word fast. ").

Phoneme blending skill has only been measured by one kind of task. This is the sound-blending task in which the tester pronounces a series of phonemes in isolation and asks the child to blend them together to form a word (i.e., "What word do these sounds make, /f/ - /a/ - /t/?"). Easier variants of the sound-blending task can be produced by allowing the child to choose from two or three pictures the word that is represented by a series of phonemes. In general, these different kinds of phonemic awareness tasks all appear to be measuring essentially the same construct, or ability. Although some researchhas indicated that the tasks may involve different levels of intellectual complexity, and there may be some differences between segmentation and blending tasks at certain ages, for the most part, they all seem to be measuring growth in the same general ability. Sound comparison measures are easiest and are sensitive to emergent levels of phonological awareness, while segmentation and blending measures are sensitive to differences among children during later stages of development involving refinements in explicit levels of awareness. Measures of sensitivity to rhyme are not included as measures of phonemic awareness because they appear to be measuring something a little different, and less predictive of reading disabilities, from those measure that ask children to attend to individual phonemes. For the same reason, measures of syllable awareness are not included in this group. Measures of phonemic awareness that are suited for early identification purposes include the following three widely used tests:

The Phonological Awareness Test. This test contains five different measures of phonemic awareness, plus a measure of sensitivity to rhyme. The five measures of phonemic awareness are segmentation of phonemes, phoneme isolation, phoneme deletion, phoneme substitution, and phoneme blending. The phoneme isolation test, which requires children to pronounce the first, last, or middle sounds in words, would appear to have the most appropriate level of difficulty for kindergarten screening (the test should be easy enough so that only the most delayed children will do poorly on it), and any of the others could be used for first- or second-grade assessments.

The Test of Phonological Awareness. This test was designed as a group-administered test of phonemic awareness for kindergarten and first-grade children. It was specifically constructed to be most sensitive to children with weaknesses in development in this area, which helps make it appropriate for identifying at-risk children. The kindergarten version of the test requires children to notice which words (represented by pictures) begin with the same first sound, while the first-grade version asks them to compare words on the basis of their last sounds. It can be easily administered to groups of five to ten children at a time.

The Yopp-Singer Test of Phoneme Segmentation is a brief test of children's ability to isolate and pronounce the individual phonemes in words. This is a task that has been widely used in research on phoneme awareness over the past twenty years, and it is highly correlated with other measures of phoneme awareness. The test was designed for children in kindergarten, but it should also be appropriate for identifying children who are weak in phonemic awareness during first grade. The test has twenty-two items that are all of the same type and that ask the child to pronounce each of the phonemes in words that vary from two to three phonemes in length.

Once reading instruction begins, the best predictor of future reading growth is current reading achievement, and the most critical indicators of good progress in learning to read during the early elementary period are measures of word reading skill. Children who end up as poor readers at the end of elementary school are almost invariably those who fail to make normal progress in these skills during the first years of elementary school. These children are most frequently impaired in both the ability to apply phonetic strategies in reading new words and in the ability to retrieve sight words from memory. They not only have difficulty becoming accurate in the application of these processes but also they frequently have special difficulties with becoming fluent in their application. Before discussing specific methods for the diagnostic assessment of these word reading skills, one general issue regarding reading assessment requires discussion. First, the assessment that will be recommended here is very different from the "authentic literacy assessment" that is currently advocated by many reading professionals. Authentic assessment is different in at least two ways from the reading assessment measures we will be discussing. First, the goal of "authentic assessment" is to measure children's application of broad literacy skills to authentic tasks, like gathering information for a report, use of literacy as a medium for social interactions, or ability to read a selection and then write a response to it. It also seeks to measure children's enjoyment, ownership, and involvement in literacy activities both at school and at home.

This kind of assessment is a clear complement to the type of assessments we will describe for monitoring growth in word level reading skills. All of the literacy outcomes that are part of authentic assessment are important parts of a total literacy assessment program. After all, if a child can read, but does not enjoy reading and does not apply important literacy skills to everyday tasks, then some important goals of literacy instruction have not been attained.

However, since these procedures are focused on high-level reading outcomes, they cannot provide precise information about level of performance on important subskills in reading. If a child's overall performance on authentic literacy tasks is limited, it is frequently difficult to obtain a precise estimate of the specific component skills that are weak. The goal of the kind of assessments we will discuss here is to quantify the degree of skill a child possesses in word identification processes that have been shown to be a critical foundation for overall reading success.Word Reading Ability

Sight word reading ability. Two measures are widely used in this area, and both involve the same assessment strategy. The Word Identification subtest from the Woodcock Reading Mastery Test-Revised and the reading subtest of the Wide Range Achievement Test-3 both require children to read lists of words that gradually increase in length and complexity while decreasing in frequency of occurrence in printed English. For example, the easiest three words on the Word Identification subtest are go, the, and me, words of mid-level difficulty are pioneer, inquire, and wealth, and the hardest three are epigraphist, facetious, and shillelagh.

Neither of these widely used tests place stringent time pressure on students, so both phonetic decoding processes and sight word processes can be used to identify words on these lists. Both tests have been normed nationally, and one of their strengths is that they allow a direct assessment of children's ability to identify words solely on the basis of the word's spelling. When reading text, children also have context clues available to assist word identification, and thus text-based measures, although they may be more "authentic" in one sense, are less direct in their assessment of the kinds of word-processing skills that are particularly deficient in children with reading problems.

Phonetic reading ability. The single best measure of children's ability to apply knowledge of letter-sound correspondences in decoding words is provided by measures of nonword reading. The Word Attack subtest of the Woodcock Reading Mastery Test-Revised is a good example of this kind of diagnostic test. It consists of a series of increasingly complex nonwords that children are asked to "sound out as best they can." The three easiest items on the test are ree, ip, and din; items of moderate difficulty are rejune, depine, and viv, and the three hardest items are pnir ceisminadolt, and byrcal. Because the words are presented out of context, they stress the child's ability to fully analyze each word to produce the correct pronunciation. On the other hand, measures such as this do not allow an assessment of children's ability to combine phonetic decoding with use of context to arrive at a word's correct pronunciation. However, since both good and poor readers appear able to use context equally well, this is not an important omission on a diagnostic measure of word reading ability.

Word reading fluency. Word reading fluency measures have typically measured rate of reading connected text. One of the more widely used measures in this area is the Gray Oral Reading Test-3rd Edition. This test consists of thirteen increasingly difficult passages, each followed by five comprehension questions. A measure of oral reading rate is obtained by recording the time it takes for the child to read each passage. One potential problem with the Gray Oral Reading Test is that it does not provide a very sensitive measure of individual differences in word reading ability at very low levels of performance, such as those found in beginning first graders, or disabled readers through second grade. The passages simply begin at too high a level for children with very poor or undeveloped reading skills to display the word reading skills they actually possess. In an effort to provide measures of fluency and accuracy in word reading skills that are simple to administer and sensitive to individual differences across a broad range of reading skills, we are currently developing simple measures of Word Reading Efficiency and Non Word Efficiency. In both of these measures, children are shown lists of increasingly difficult words and nonwords and asked to read as many words as possible in forty-five seconds. There are two forms to each test, and the child's score is simply the average number of words read in forty-five seconds. Initial evaluations indicate that these measures are very reliable.They are also highly correlated with corresponding measures from the Woodcock Reading Mastery Test-Revised at early grades and slightly less correlated at fourth grade, when fluency of word reading processes becomes more important to performance on the tests. If a single form of each test is administered, it will provide indices of growth in phonetic decoding and sight word reading that can be administered several times during the year and that take a very short amount of time to give.

Collaborative Classroom

Beginning reading instruction has been significantly influenced by two seemingly incompatible bodies of research, one advocating a strong focus on meaning and the other advocating for direct instruction in phoneme awareness. The dichotomy is perpetuated when general educators are trained in holistic teaching methods and special educators are trained in direct instruction methods. Neither method is wrong for the purpose for which it was developed; on the other hand, neither method is the right one for all children. However, one of the most consistent findings to emerge from the past decade of research on reading is the relationships among phoneme awareness, reading acquisition, and later reading success. The findings strongly suggest that children who lack phoneme awareness skills as a precursor to learning to read are at risk for developing reading disabilities and need explicit instruction in phoneme awareness if they are to become skilled readers and spellers.

Techniques that target phoneme awareness most frequently involve direct instruction in segmenting words into component sounds, identifying sounds in various positions in words (initial, medial, final), identifying words that begin or end with the same sound, and manipulating sounds in a word such as saying a word without its beginning or end sound. Because a fundamental tenet of the whole language approach to reading instruction is that word analysis skills should only arise incidentally in the context of reading connected text, some teachers resist incorporating systematic phoneme awareness activities into their reading programs. Unfortunately, most kindergarten reading-readiness programs also do not incorporate systematic phoneme awareness components. Although special education teachers have the requisite background in direct instruction, the students most in need of this instruction- young beginning readers lacking phoneme awareness skills- are usually found in general education classrooms. Systematic instruction needs to be skillfully implemented in a collaborative effort with the general education teacher.

Skillful implementation assumes the integration of phoneme awareness activities in meaningful contexts and in conjunction with the reading approach being used in the classroom. The selected activities are primarily for whole class participation, although they can be used on an individual or small- group basis and can be adapted for older students who are struggling with reading.

Most of the phoneme awareness activities should not take more than 15 or 20 minutes to complete and should fit the context of the classroom. Although a particular activity can be selected well in advance, the specific words targeted for phoneme awareness should be selected from material used actively in the class, such as a story or picture book that was just read and discussed, the immediate environment, words fitting a thematic unit being taught, or discussions about a field trip. Phoneme awareness activities work well in classrooms where teachers implement shared reading. Typically, after previewing the text with the class, the teacher reads aloud a large- print text on a chart or in a big book, the teacher and children read the selection together, and then students complete individual activities related to the selection. Phoneme awareness activities are a natural extension of the shared reading activities. To be successful, however, the general educator and special educator must plan ahead for sharing time, space, and teaching together in a collaborative effort.

The benefits for the children far outweigh any disadvantages for the teachers. The willingness of the special educator to fit the activities to the contexts of the classroom can help diminish any existing reluctance a general education teacher might have toward phoneme awareness training. Phonograms are the common elements in word families (e.g., the letter sequence "and" in sand, hand, band, and land). The initial consonant that changes the meaning of the word is called an onset and the following vowel/consonant combination that remains constant is called a rime. Because an awareness of syllables, onsets, and rimes develops before an awareness of phonemes, the first set of suggestions focuses on ways to expose children to word play.

A natural and spontaneous way of providing children with exposure to phonemes is to focus on literature that deals playfully with speech sounds through rhymes. Simple rhyme patterns are easily recalled after repeated exposure, and children will get the idea of creating new rhymes. Assonance, the repetition of vowel sounds within words, is often combined with rhyme, as in "It rains and hails and shakes the sails" from "Sheep on a Ship" or in humorous ways such as "The tooter tries to tutor two tooters to toot" in "Moses Supposes His Toeses Are Roses". Some books include music to go with the rhymes, such as "Down by the Bay", in which two children try to outdo one another in making up questions that rhyme, such as "Did you ever see a goose kissing a moose?" Yopp presented an annotated bibliography of 44 books for young children that deal playfully with language. She also provided guidelines for using these books in class: (a) read and reread the stories; (b) comment on the language use; (c) encourage predictions of sound, word, and sentence patterns; (d) comment on or elicit specific aspects of sound patterns; and (e) be creative in inventing new versions of the language patterns utilized in the stories.

Word Families Chart

The exposure to rhymes leads naturally to the use of phonograms and the creation of word family charts. Charts can contain words from one story or a brain- stormed list from the children. A story that leads naturally to a word family chart is "Tog the Dog", which is constructed so that as each page is turned, a different letter lines up with the rime "og." For example, when Tog takes a jog, the letter "j" lines up with the "og." The children can dictate to the teacher words to be placed on a word family chart. As they begin to develop letter/sound knowledge, they can copy or write the words themselves. You can use magnetic letters to "create" words for a word family chart. Provide a rime of plastic letters (e.g., at) and have the children take turns placing different letters in the onset position to create new words (e.g., hat, bat, sat, rat). These charts can be used as reference charts (or the children can make their own word families reference book) for spelling and creative writing activities.

Direct Instruction

Children who are struggling with recognizing and creating rhymed words may need more direct intervention. Initial rhyme recognition can be reinforced by direct modeling of instances (nose- rose) and non-instances (bed- car) of rhyming word pairs. The children are then presented other word pairs and asked if the two words sound the same or sound different. This can be made into a game-like activity by having them respond with a "happy face" card if the words rhyme and a "sad face" card if they don't (or they can use a "thumbs up" and "thumbs down" response). It is important for the teacher to ask a child to repeat the rhyming pairs in this and the following activities to reinforce the verbal production of rhymed words.

Pictures provide visual cues for rhyme recognition and can be used during the modeling phase of instruction. The teacher can then present three pictures and ask the child to select and say the two that rhyme. A variation would be to display two nonrhyming pictures and have the child select the one that rhymes with the word being said by the teacher. Bradley and Bryant used an activity called "Odd Word Out," which can be done with or without pictures. Four words, three of which rhyme, are presented by the teacher (e.g., zveed, bead, pill, seed). The child determines which word is the odd one that doesn't belong with the others.

The game of concentration or memory is a good practice activity for rhyme recognition. Separate pictures (not printed words) of rhyming word pairs (e.g., cat/bat) are shuffled, and all are placed facedown in a grid pattern. The children take turns turning two cards faceup, trying to match a rhyme pair. If a match is made, the child keeps that pair and takes another turn. If not, the cards are turned facedown and the next child gets a turn.

As stated by Lewkowicz, "Children should be familiarized with speech sounds in isolation before they attempt to detect sounds within words". Because children are usually unaware that words are made up of individual speech sounds that can be produced in isolation, it is up to the teacher to provide children with a concept of speech sounds. This is probably best done by associating phonemes with a creature, an action, or an object that is familiar to the child. For example, the phoneme /s/ can be associated with the hissing sound a snake makes-ssssss. Many sounds have natural associations, such as a crowing rooster for /r/, a buzzing bee for /z/, and the "be quiet" sound for /sh/. Sound personalities can be introduced naturally and in context by selecting a particular sound to talk about that is stressed in alphabet or other books that use alliteration. For example, Obligato presented "smiling snakes sipping strawberry sodas" for the alphabet letter S.

It is helpful to create or provide pictures that represent these sound personalities and to post them in the room as each is introduced. A natural connection can sometimes be made between the sound and the letter, such as presenting a picture of "Sammy snake" drawn in the shape of the letter S or "Buzzy bee" flying in a pattern of the letter Z Besides providing a label to facilitate talking about sounds, the pictures provide self-correcting cues for children engaged in initialsound isolation and sound-to-word matching activities.

Word counting can be done for any sentence selected from a reading or writing lesson. The sentence should be read to the children without being visible. The children listen and place a marker from left to right for each word heard. The teacher can confirm the number of words by showing the printed sentence to the children, pointing to each word as it is read, and having the children touch their tokens in one- to- one correspondence. Or the teacher can reinforce the children's "counting" using auditory input only by repeating the sentence and having them touch each token to confirm the number of words heard. To count syllables in words, activities can be used such as clapping hands, tapping the desk, or marching in place to the syllables in children's names (Ma- ry), items in the immediate environment (win- dow), or words from a favorite story (wi-shy, wa-shy). Initially, two- syllable words can be targeted, building up to three. Visible, manipulable representation of sounds also helps to clarify and guide counting and segmentation tasks for beginners. The marker activity used for word counting can be adapted for use in counting syllables by providing each child with two or three horizontally connected boxes drawn on a sheet of paper. The children place a token in each box from left to right as they hear each syllable in a word. These same activities can be used to count sounds in words.

Sound synthesis or sound blending is an essential skill related to later reading ability and one of the easiest phoneme awareness tasks for children to perform. Sound synthesis can be done using the following sequence: blending an initial sound onto the remainder of a word, followed by blending syllables of a word together, and then blending isolated phonemes into a word. The teacher can model blending an initial sound onto a word by using the jingle "It starts with /1/ and it ends with ight, put it together, and it says light." When they have the idea, the children supply the final word. An element of excitement can be created by using children's names for this activity and asking each child to recognize and say his or her own name when it is presented- "It starts with /b/ and it ends with etsy, put it together and it says — — — —." Context can be provided by limiting the words to objects that can be seen in the room or to words from a particular story the children just read. As the children become proficient, they can take turns using the jingle to present their own words to be blended by the class. Guessing games that utilize words broken into syllables or isolated phonemes provide fun sound blending activities. One involves using a puppet (perhaps representing a character from a current reading lesson) who speaks "funny" by saying words syllable- by- syllable or sound- by- sound for the children to figure out. Initial clues can be provided by displaying three pictures, one of which is the word being said by the puppet.

The puppet can confirm or negate a student response by picking up the picture and saying the word being segmented: "/f/-/i/-/sh/ ... I said fish!" Another is the familiar "What's in the bag?" activity. Instead of describing what is in the bag, the teacher says the word syllable- by- syllable or sound- by- sound and the children guess the word.

Sound- to- word matching is useful as a beginning step in sound segmentation. Basically, sound- to- word matching requires that the child identify the beginning sound of a word. Awareness of the initial sound in a word can be done by showing the children a picture (dog) and asking the children to identify the correct word out of three: "Is this a /mmm/-og, a /d/d/d/-og, or a /sss/-og?" A variation is to ask if the word has a particular sound: "Is there a /d/ in dog?" This can then be switched to "Which sound does dog start with-/d/, /sh/, or /1/?" This sequence encourages the children to try out the three onsets with the rime to see which one is correct. It is easiest to use continuants that can be exaggerated and prolonged to heighten the sound input. Iteration should be used with stop consonants to add emphasis.

The children might use favorite stories from their reading lessons to identify different sets of three words that start with the same sound to incorporate into the song. Each repeated verse could then emphasize a different sound. The teacher again is cautioned to use the phoneme sounds, not the letter names for these activities.

Establishing that sounds occur in different positions of words- initial, final, and medial- helps some children with the later task of segmenting whole words into isolated sound components. One method of representing sound positions is to display a picture of a train composed of an engine, a passenger car, and a caboose. Three connecting boxes can be drawn under each component: one under the engine, connected to one under the passenger car, connected to the one under the caboose (use poster board and laminate). Explain that words have beginning, middle, and end sounds just like the train has a beginning, a middle, and an end part. Demonstrate by slowly articulating a CVC (consonant- vowel- consonant word (e.g., /p/ ... /i/ ... /g/) and pointing to the box corresponding to the position of each sound in the word. You can then repeat the word and ask the children to identify where they hear the different sounds – "Where do you hear the /g/ in pig/" Slowly articulate other CVC words for them to listen to and have them mark the box under the train that indicates the position of the sound you specify.

Segmenting refers to the act of isolating the sounds in a spoken word by separately pronouncing each one in order. Yopp stated that segmenting the sounds in a word is one of the more difficult simple phonemic tasks for children to perform. Lewkowicz and Yopp suggested starting with isolated productions of initial phonemes as a precursor to segmenting entire words. The previous sound-to- word matching and identification of position activities help in early recognition and practice with initial phonemes. Several researchers have used visual and tactile cues based on Elkonin boxes to help with phoneme segmentation.

A card is prepared with a picture of a simple word at the top. Below the picture is a matrix that contains a box for each phoneme (not letter) in the word (Figure 1 below). The teacher models the process by slowing articulating the word phoneme- by - phoneme while pushing a counter into a box for each phoneme. The children can say the word with the teacher while the counters are being placed. Gradually the children should participate in this "say it and move it" activity by taking turns placing the counters in each box while saying each sound in a word. Both the matrix and picture can be eliminated over time so that the children are segmenting the word without visual clues. Words should be selected from familiar text to ensure a whole- to- part sequence of instruction and to provide the children with contextual cues that link word segmentation to everyday classroom lessons.

Many researchers have demonstrated the advantage of combining phoneme awareness with letter knowledge in a classroom setting. The most pedagogically sound method of phoneme awareness training is one that eventually makes explicit the complete letter- to- sound mappings in segmented words. All phoneme awareness activities that use tokens or other visual representations of sounds can be modified to include letter- sound associations. As individual sounds are mastered by the children, their corresponding letter names can be introduced and placed on the tokens and gradually introduced into the segmentation activities.

At first, only one letter or tile should be provided, and the remainder should be blank. After the child has successfully segmented with one letter or tile, others can be added as new letter names are mastered. To reinforce letter names, Blachman played "post office" — the children slect a picture, say the initial sound of the picture, and identify the letter represented by the first sound by "mailing" it in the appropriate letter pouch. A modified game of bingo can provide practice in sound- letter association. The desired letters to be emphasized are selected, starting with two or three, and adding more as the children progress.

The letters are printed in random order on cards that have 4- by- 4 or 5- by- 5 grids drawn on them, one card for each child. The teacher draws from a container letter tiles matching those on the children's cards. The teacher says the phoneme for the letter drawn from the container (replacing it each time) and asks the children to identify the letter corresponding to the phoneme by placing a marker in the appropriate box on their cards. Any child who fills a row or column can then name the letters aloud. The practice of invented spelling in a classroom can also be used to make explicit connections between sound segments and letters. Children select words they wish to write but don't know how to spell. A box is drawn for each sound in the word (remember that one sound may be represented by two or more letters- the word shoes, for example, has only three phonemes, /sh/-/oo/-/z/). A child can fill in the letters he or she hears and knows with the teacher's help. The teacher can fill in any letters the child does not know.

Word-to-Word Matching

Compound phonemic awareness requires holding a given sound in memory while performing a second operation such as determining whether two words begin with the same sound in a word- to-word matching task. Byrne offered several games for practicing word- to- word matching.

1. Make a set of dominoes that have two pictured objects on each card. The children are required to join cards sharing beginning (or ending) sounds.

2. A version of "snap" uses cards having one picture. The children take turns drawing a card from a face-down pile and placing it in a face-up pile. When a newly drawn card has the same beginning (or end) sound as the top card in the face-up pile, the first child to identify the match by saying "snap" collects the pile.

3. Sound bingo uses bingo cards with pictures that children mark if one of their pictures has the same beginning (or end) sound as the word said by the caller.

Each of these games can be related to other classroom activities by having the children make their own dominoes, snap cards, and bingo cards using pictures cut from catalogs or magazines, or hand drawn and laminated. The pictures selected by the children can represent things related to the literature and themes being covered in class.

Sound Deletion

Because sound deletion tasks require manipulation of phonemes in words, they are considered to be more difficult than other types of phoneme awareness tasks. Cole and Mengler stated that it is not until a mental age of approximately 7 years that children are able to perform phoneme deletion tasks adequately. Lewkowicz suggested that sound deletion activities be done after the children exhibit some skill in segmentation and after letter names have been introduced. Because phoneme deletion of medial consonants puts an undue burden on young children's memory, sound deletion should target only initial or final sounds in words. To introduce the idea of deleting parts of a word, the teacher can show pictures or point to objects in the room that are compound words and demonstrate how each word can be said with a part missing.

Identification of a missing sound can be accomplished through a "What's missing? " guessing game. The teacher says two words for comparison and asks the children to identify the missing element: "Listen: eat-meat. What's missing in eat that you can hear in meat?" Final position deletions can be done in the same way (e.g., "What's missing in play that you can hear in plane?"). The children can be encouraged to make up their own "What's missing?" words for the initial position by referring to the phonograms on the word families charts: "What's missing in an that you can hear in pan (man, ran, can)." Identifying the missing element using phonograms tends to be easier than using unrelated words because the initial consonant determines the meaning of the word for the child and the rime remains constant.

9

Teaching Speaking and Listening

Speaking, its form and meaning are dependent on the context in which it occurs, including the participants themselves, their collective experiences, the physical environment, and the purposes for speaking. It is often spontaneous, open-ended, and evolving. However, speech is not always unpredictable. Language functions (or patterns) that tend to recur in certain discourse situations (e.g., declining an invitation or requesting time off from work), can be identified and charted. For example, when a salesperson asks "May I help you?" the expected discourse sequence includes a statement of need, response to the need, offer of appreciation, acknowledgement of the appreciation, and a leave-taking exchange.

Speaking requires that learners not only know how to produce specific points of language such as grammar, pronunciation, or vocabulary *(linguistic competence)*, but also that they understand when, why, and in what ways to produce language *(sociolinguistic competence)*. Finally, speech has its own skills, structures, and conventions different from written language. A good speaker synthesizes this array of skills and knowledge to succeed in a given speech act. A speaker's skills and speech habits have an impact on the success of any exchange.

Speakers must be able to anticipate and then produce the expected patterns of specific discourse situations. They must also manage discrete elements such as turn-taking, rephrasing, providing feedback, or redirecting. For example, a learner involved in the exchange with the salesperson described previously must know the usual pattern that such an interaction follows and access that knowledge as the exchange progresses. The learner must also choose the correct vocabulary to describe the item sought, rephrase or emphasize words to clarify the description if the clerk does not understand, and use appropriate facial expressions to indicate satisfaction or dissatisfaction with the service. Other skills and knowledge that instruction might address include the following:

- producing the sounds, stress patterns, rhythmic structures, and intonations of the language;
- using grammar structures accurately;
- assessing characteristics of the target audience, including shared knowledge or shared points of reference, status and power relations of participants, interest levels, or differences in perspectives;
- selecting vocabulary that is understandable and appropriate for the audience, the topic being discussed, and the setting in which the speech act occurs;
- applying strategies to enhance comprehensibility, such as emphasizing key words, rephrasing, or checking for listener comprehension;
- using gestures or body language; and
- paying attention to the success of the interaction and adjusting components of speech such as vocabulary, rate of speech, and complexity of grammar structures to maximize listener comprehension and involvement.

Many language learners regard speaking ability as the measure of knowing a language. These learners define fluency as the ability to converse with others, much more than the ability to read, write, or comprehend oral language. They regard speaking as the most important skill they can acquire, and they assess their progress in terms of their accomplishments in spoken communication.

Language learners need to recognize that speaking involves three areas of knowledge:

- Mechanics (pronunciation, grammar, and vocabulary): Using the right words in the right order with the correct pronunciation
- Functions (transaction and interaction): Knowing when clarity of message is essential (transaction/information exchange) and when precise understanding is not required (interaction/relationship building)
- Social and cultural rules and norms (turn-taking, rate of speech, length of pauses between speakers, relative roles of participants): Understanding how to take into account who is speaking to whom, in what circumstances, about what, and for what reason.

In the communicative model of language teaching, instructors help their students develop this body of knowledge by providing authentic practice that prepares students for real-life communication situations. They help their students develop the ability to produce grammatically correct, logically connected sentences that are appropriate to specific contexts, and to do so using acceptable (that is, comprehensible) pronunciation.

The goal of teaching speaking skills is communicative efficiency. Learners should be able to make themselves understood, using their current proficiency to the fullest.

They should try to avoid confusion in the message due to faulty pronunciation, grammar, or vocabulary, and to observe the social and cultural rules that apply in each communication situation.

To help students develop communicative efficiency in speaking, instructors can use a balanced activities approach that combines language input, structured output, and communicative output.

Language input comes in the form of teacher talk, listening activities, reading passages, and the language heard and read outside of class. It gives learners the material they need to begin producing language themselves.

Language input may be content oriented or form oriented.

— Content-oriented input focuses on information, whether it is a simple weather report or an extended lecture on an academic topic. Content-oriented input may also include descriptions of learning strategies and examples of their use.

— Form-oriented input focuses on ways of using the language: guidance from the teacher or another source on vocabulary, pronunciation, and grammar (linguistic competence); appropriate things to say in specific contexts (discourse competence); expectations for rate of speech, pause length, turn-taking, and other social aspects of language use (sociolinguistic competence); and explicit instruction in phrases to use to ask for clarification and repair miscommunication (strategic competence).

In the presentation part of a lesson, an instructor combines content-oriented and form-oriented input. The amount of input that is actually provided in the target language depends on students' listening proficiency and also on the situation. For students at lower levels, or in situations where a quick explanation on a grammar topic is needed, an explanation in English may be more appropriate than one in the target language. Structured output focuses on correct form. In structured output, students may have options for responses, but all of the options require them to use the specific form or structure that the teacher has just introduced. Structured output is designed to make learners comfortable producing specific language items recently introduced, sometimes in combination with previously learned items. Instructors often use structured output exercises as a transition between the presentation stage and the practice stage of a lesson plan. textbook exercises also often make good structured output practice activities.

In communicative output, the learners' main purpose is to complete a task, such as obtaining information, developing a travel plan, or creating a video. To complete the task, they may use the language that the instructor has just presented, but they also may draw on any other vocabulary, grammar, and communication strategies that they know. In communicative output activities, the criterion of success is whether the learner gets the message across. Accuracy is not a consideration unless the lack of it interferes with the message. In everyday communication, spoken exchanges take place because there is some sort of information gap between the participants. Communicative output activities involve a similar real information gap. In order to complete the task, students must reduce or eliminate the information gap. In these activities, language is a tool, not an end in itself. In a balanced activities approach, the teacher uses a variety of activities from these different categories of input and output. Learners at all proficiency levels, including beginners, benefit from this variety; it is more motivating, and it is also more likely to result in effective language learning.

Developing Speaking Skills

Students often think that the ability to speak a language is the product of language learning, but speaking is also a crucial part of the language learning process. Effective instructors teach students speaking strategies – using minimal responses, recognizing scripts, and using language to talk about language – that they can use to help themselves expand their knowledge of the language and their confidence in using it. These instructors help students learn to speak so that the students can use speaking to learn.

Language learners who lack confidence in their ability to participate successfully in oral interaction often listen in silence while others do the talking. One way to encourage such learners to begin to participate is to help them build up a stock of minimal responses that they can use in different types of exchanges. Such responses can be especially useful for beginners. Minimal responses are predictable, often idiomatic phrases that conversation participants use to indicate understanding, agreement, doubt, and other responses to what another speaker is saying. Having a stock of such responses enables a learner to focus on what the other participant is saying, without having to simultaneously plan a response.

Instructors can help students develop speaking ability by making them aware of the scripts for different situations so that they can predict what they will hear and what they will need to say in response. Through interactive activities, instructors can give students practice in managing and varying the language that different scripts contain.

Language learners are often too embarrassed or shy to say anything when they do not understand another speaker or when they realize that a conversation partner has not understood them. Instructors can help students overcome this reticence by assuring them that misunderstanding and the need for clarification can occur in any type of interaction, whatever the participants' language skill levels. Instructors can also give students strategies and phrases to use for clarification and comprehension check. By encouraging students to use clarification phrases in class when misunderstanding occurs, and by responding positively when they do, instructors can create an authentic practice environment within the classroom itself. As they develop control of various clarification strategies, students will gain confidence in their ability to manage the various communication situations that they may encounter outside the classroom.

Oral Communication Skills

Communicative and whole language instructional approaches promote integration of speaking, listening, reading, and writing in ways that reflect natural language use. But opportunities for speaking and listening require structure and planning if they are to support language development.

Outside the classroom, listening is used twice as often as speaking, which in turn is used twice as much as reading and writing. Inside the classroom, speaking and listening are the most often used skills . These skills are also logical instructional starting points when learners have low literacy levels or limited formal education, or when they come from language backgrounds with a non-Roman script or a predominantly oral tradition. Further, with the drive to incorporate workforce readiness skills into adult instruction, practice time is being devoted to such speaking skills as reporting, negotiating, clarifying, and problem solving.

Speaking lessons can follow the usual pattern of preparation, presentation, practice, evaluation, and extension.

The teacher can use the *preparation* step to establish a context for the speaking task (where, when, why, and with whom it will occur) and to initiate awareness of the speaking skill to be targeted (asking for clarification, stressing key words, using reduced forms of words).

In *presentation*, the teacher can provide learners with a preproduction model that furthers learner comprehension and helps them become more attentive observers of language use.

Practice involves learners in reproducing the targeted structure, usually in a controlled or highly supported manner.

Evaluation involves directing attention to the skill being examined and asking learners to monitor and assess their own progress. Finally, *extension* consists of activities that ask learners to use the strategy or skill in a different context or authentic communicative situation, or to integrate use of the new skill or strategy with previously acquired ones.

Choosing appropriate topics for small talk

1. *Preparation*. Show the learners a picture of two people conversing in a familiar casual setting. (The setting will be determined by a prior needs assessment.) Ask them to brainstorm what the people might be discussing (i.e., what topics, vocabulary, typical phrases).

2. *Presentation.* Present several video clips of small talk in casual situations. Have learners complete a worksheet in which they describe or list the topics discussed, the context in which the speech is occurring, and any phrases that seem to typify small talk. Follow up with a discussion of the kinds of topics that are appropriate for small talk, the factors in the specific situations that affect topic selection (e.g., relationships of participants, physical setting), and typical phrases used in small talk. Chart this information.

3. *Practice.* Give learners specific information about the participants and the setting of a scenario where small talk will take place. In pairs, have them list topics that might be discussed by the participants and simple phrases they might use. Learners then engage in improvised dialogues based on these simple phrases.

4. *Evaluation.* Give pairs a teacher-prepared dialogue based on their scenario from. Ask them to compare their improvised dialogues with the prepared dialogue, analyzing the similarities, differences, and reasons for both.

5. *Extension.* Have learners go individually or in small groups into various contexts in the community and record the conversations they hear. Ask them to report their findings back to the class, and then have the class discuss these findings.

In-class speaking tasks

Although dialogues and conversations are the most obvious and most often used speaking activities in language classrooms, a teacher can select activities from a variety of tasks. Brown lists six possible task categories:

- *Imitative:* Drills in which the learner simply repeats a phrase or structure (e.g., "Excuse me." or "Can you help me?") for clarity and accuracy;
- *Intensive:* Drills or repetitions focusing on specific phonological or grammatical points, such as minimal pairs or repetition of a series of imperative sentences;
- *Responsive:* Short replies to teacher or learner questions or comments, such as a series of answers to yes/no questions;
- *Transactional:* Dialogues conducted for the purpose of information exchange, such as information-gathering interviews, role plays, or debates;
- *Interpersonal:* Dialogues to establish or maintain social relationships, such as personal interviews or casual conversation role plays; and
- *Extensive:* Extended monologues such as short speeches, oral reports, or oral summaries.

These tasks are not sequential. Each can be used independently or they can be integrated with one another, depending on learners' needs. For example, if learners are not using appropriate sentence intonations when participating in a *transactional* activity that focuses on the skill of politely interrupting to make a point, the teacher might decide to follow up with a brief *imitative* lesson targeting this feature.

When presenting tasks, teachers should tell learners about the language function to be produced in the task and the real context(s) in which it usually occurs. They should provide opportunities for interactive practice and build upon previous instruction as necessary. Teachers should also be careful not to overload a speaking lesson with other new material such as numerous vocabulary or grammatical structures. This can distract learners from the primary speaking goals of the lesson.

Traditional classroom speaking practice often takes the form of drills in which one person asks a question and another gives an answer. The question and the answer are structured and predictable, and often there is only one correct, predetermined answer. The purpose of asking and answering the question is to demonstrate the ability to ask and answer the question.

In contrast, the purpose of real communication is to accomplish a task, such as conveying a telephone message, obtaining information, or expressing an opinion. In real communication, participants must manage uncertainty about what the other person will say. Authentic communication involves an information gap; each participant has information that the other does not have. In addition, to achieve their purpose, participants may have to clarify their meaning or ask for confirmation of their own understanding.

To create classroom speaking activities that will develop communicative competence, instructors need to incorporate a purpose and an information gap and allow for multiple forms of expression. However, quantity alone will not necessarily produce competent speakers. Instructors need to combine structured output activities, which allow for error correction and increased accuracy, with communicative output activities that give students opportunities to practice language use more freely.

Two common kinds of structured output activities are *information gap* and *jigsaw* activities. In both these types of activities, students complete a task by obtaining missing information, a feature the activities have in common with real communication. However, information gap and jigsaw activities also set up practice on specific items of language. In this respect they are more like drills than like communication.

The aim of speaking is communication and that does not require perfect language, then it makes sense to encourage quantity in your classroom. Break the silence and get students communicating with whatever language they can use, correct or not, and selectively address errors that block communication.

Speaking lessons often tie in pronunciation and grammar which are necessary for effective oral communication. Or a grammar or reading lesson may incorporate a speaking activity. Either way, your students will need some preparation before the speaking task. This includes introducing the topic and providing a model of the speech they are to produce. A model may not apply to discussion-type activities, in which case students will need clear and specific instructions about the task to be accomplished. Then the students will practice with the actual speaking activity. These activities may include imitating (repeating), answering verbal cues, interactive conversation, or an oral presentation. Most speaking activities inherently practice listening skills as well, such as when one student is given a simple drawing and sits behind another student, facing away. The first must give instructions to the second to reproduce the drawing. The second student asks questions to clarify unclear instructions, and neither can look at each other's page during the activity. Information gaps are also commonly used for speaking practice, as are surveys, discussions, and role-plays. Speaking activities abound; see the Activities and Further Resources sections of this guide for ideas.

Here are some ideas to keep in mind as you plan your speaking activities.

— *Content*: As much as possible, the content should be practical and usable in real-life situations. Avoid too much new vocabulary or grammar, and focus on speaking with the language the students have.

— *Correcting Errors*: You need to provide appropriate feedback and correction, but don't interrupt the flow of communication. Take notes while pairs or groups are talking and address problems to the class after the activity without embarrassing the student who made the error. You can write the error on the board and ask who can correct it.

— *Quantity vs. Quality*: Address both interactive fluency and accuracy, striving foremost for communication. Get to know each learner's personality and encourage the quieter ones to take more risks.

— *Conversation Strategies*: Encourage strategies like asking for clarification, paraphrasing, gestures, and initiating.

— Teacher Intervention: If a speaking activity loses steam, you may need to jump into a role-play, ask more discussion questions, clarify your instructions, or stop an activity that is too difficult or boring.

Information Gap Activities

— *Filling the gaps in a schedule or timetable*: Partner A holds an airline timetable with some of the arrival and departure times missing. Partner B has the same timetable but with different blank spaces. The two partners are not permitted to see each other's timetables and must fill in the blanks by asking each other appropriate questions. The features of language that are practiced would include questions beginning with "when" or "at what time." Answers would be limited mostly to time expressions like "at 8:15" or "at ten in the evening."

– *Completing the picture*: The two partners have similar pictures, each with different missing details, and they cooperate to find all the missing details. In another variation, no items are missing, but similar items differ in appearance. For example, in one picture, a man walking along the street may be wearing an overcoat, while in the other the man is wearing a jacket. The features of grammar and vocabulary that are practiced are determined by the content of the pictures and the items that are missing or different. Differences in the activities depicted lead to practice of different verbs. Differences in number, size, and shape lead to adjective practice. Differing locations would probably be described with prepositional phrases.

These activities may be set up so that the partners must practice more than just grammatical and lexical features. For example, the timetable activity gains a social dimension when one partner assumes the role of a student trying to make an appointment with a partner who takes the role of a professor. Each partner has pages from an appointment book in which certain dates and times are already filled in and other times are still available for an appointment. Of course, the open times don't match exactly, so there must be some polite negotiation to arrive at a mutually convenient time for a meeting or a conference.

Jigsaw Activities

Jigsaw activities are more elaborate information gap activities that can be done with several partners. In a jigsaw activity, each partner has one or a few pieces of the "puzzle," and the partners must cooperate to fit all the pieces into a whole picture. The puzzle piece may take one of several forms. It may be one panel from a comic strip or one photo from a set that tells a story. It may be one sentence from a written narrative. It may be a tape recording of a conversation, in which case no two partners hear exactly the same conversation.

In one fairly simple jigsaw activity, students work in groups of four. Each student in the group receives one panel from a comic strip. Partners may not show each other their panels. Together the four panels present this narrative: a man takes a container of ice cream from the freezer; he serves himself several scoops of ice cream; he sits in front of the TV eating his ice cream; he returns with the empty bowl to the kitchen and finds that he left the container of ice cream, now melting, on the kitchen counter. These pictures have a clear narrative line and the partners are not likely to disagree about the appropriate sequencing. You can make the task more demanding, however, by using pictures that lend themselves to alternative sequences, so that the partners have to negotiate among themselves to agree on a satisfactory sequence.

More elaborate jigsaws may proceed in two stages. Students first work in input groups (groups A, B, C, and D) to receive information. Each group receives a different part of the total information for the task. Students then reorganize into groups of four with one student each from A, B, C, and D, and use the information they received to complete the task. Such an organization could be used, for example, when the input is given in the form of a tape recording. Groups A, B, C, and D each hear a different recording of a short news bulletin. The four recordings all contain the same general information, but each has one or more details that the others do not. In the second stage, students reconstruct the complete story by comparing the four versions.

With information gap and jigsaw activities, instructors need to be conscious of the language demands they place on their students. If an activity calls for language your students have not already practiced, you can brainstorm with them when setting up the activity to preview the language they will need, eliciting what they already know and supplementing what they are able to produce themselves.

Structured output activities can form an effective bridge between instructor modeling and communicative output because they are partly authentic and partly artificial. Like authentic communication, they feature information gaps that must be bridged for successful completion of the task.

However, where authentic communication allows speakers to use all of the language they know, structured output activities lead students to practice specific features of language and to practice only in brief sentences, not in extended discourse. Also, structured output situations are contrived and more like games than real communication, and the participants' social roles are irrelevant to the performance of the activity. This structure controls the number of variables that students must deal with when they are first exposed to new material. As they become comfortable, they can move on to true communicative output activities.

Communicative Output Activities

Communicative output activities allow students to practice using all of the language they know in situations that resemble real settings. In these activities, students must work together to develop a plan, resolve a problem, or complete a task. The most common types of communicative output activity are *role plays* and *discussions*.

In role plays, students are assigned roles and put into situations that they may eventually encounter outside the classroom. Because role plays imitate life, the range of language functions that may be used expands considerably. Also, the role relationships among the students as they play their parts call for them to practice and develop their sociolinguistic competence. They have to use language that is appropriate to the situation and to the characters.

Students usually find role playing enjoyable, but students who lack self-confidence or have lower proficiency levels may find them intimidating at first. To succeed with role plays:

– *Prepare carefully:* Introduce the activity by describing the situation and making sure that all of the students understand it

– *Set a goal or outcome*: Be sure the students understand what the product of the role play should be, whether a plan, a schedule, a group opinion, or some other product

– *Use role cards:* Give each student a card that describes the person or role to be played. For lower-level students, the cards can include words or expressions that that person might use.

– *Brainstorm:* Before you start the role play, have students brainstorm as a class to predict what vocabulary, grammar, and idiomatic expressions they might use.

- *Keep groups small:* Less-confident students will feel more able to participate if they do not have to compete with many voices.
- *Give students time to prepare*: Let them work individually to outline their ideas and the language they will need to express them.
- *Be present as a resource, not a monitor:* Stay in communicative mode to answer students' questions. Do not correct their pronunciation or grammar unless they specifically ask you about it.
- *Allow students to work at their own levels*: Each student has individual language skills, an individual approach to working in groups, and a specific role to play in the activity. Do not expect all students to contribute equally to the discussion, or to use every grammar point you have taught.
- *Do topical follow-up:* Have students report to the class on the outcome of their role plays.
- *Do linguistic follow-up:* After the role play is over, give feedback on grammar or pronunciation problems you have heard. This can wait until another class period when you plan to review pronunciation or grammar anyway.
- Discussions, like role plays, succeed when the instructor prepares students first, and then gets out of the way. To succeed with discussions:
- *Prepare the students:* Give them input (both topical information and language forms) so that they will have something to say and the language with which to say it.

– *Offer choices:* Let students suggest the topic for discussion or choose from several options. Discussion does not always have to be about serious issues. Students are likely to be more motivated to participate if the topic is television programs, plans for a vacation, or news about mutual friends. Weighty topics like how to combat pollution are not as engaging and place heavy demands on students' linguistic competence.

– *Set a goal or outcome*: This can be a group product, such as a letter to the editor, or individual reports on the views of others in the group.

– *Use small groups instead of whole-class discussion:* Large groups can make participation difficult.

– *Keep it short*: Give students a defined period of time, not more than 8-10 minutes, for discussion. Allow them to stop sooner if they run out of things to say.

– *Allow students to participate in their own way:* Not every student will feel comfortable talking about every topic. Do not expect all of them to contribute equally to the conversation.

Through well-prepared communicative output activities such as role plays and discussions, you can encourage students to experiment and innovate with the language, and create a supportive atmosphere that allows them to make mistakes without fear of embarrassment. This will contribute to their self-confidence as speakers and to their motivation to learn more.

Teaching Speaking: Suggestions for the Classroom

In speaking classes students must be exposed to three key items:

(1) form-focused instruction, that is, attention to details of pronunciation, grammar, vocabulary, and so forth;

(2) meaning-focused instruction, that is, opportunities to produce meaningful spoken messages with real communicative purposes; and

(3) opportunities to improve fluency. Elements of all of the above should be present throughout a speaking program, with emphasis on form-focused instruction at the elementary levels and, as the learners progress, on meaning-focused instruction at the higher levels.

Form-focused Speaking

When learners first begin to speak in another language their speaking will need to be based on some form-focused learning. An effective way to begin is to base speaking on some useful, simple memorized phrases and sentences. These may be greetings, simple personal descriptions, and simple questions and answers. These can be practiced in Repetition drills. The teacher says a phrase or sentence several times and then asks the learners to repeat. Some learners can be called on to repeat individually, and then the class may repeat together. Because it is helpful to give learners quite a lot of repetition practice in beginning level courses, the teacher needs to find ways of varying repetition activities to keep the learners interested. Here is a list of possible ways to vary repetition. As an example, use the sentence "Where is the train station?"

1. *The teacher varies the speed.* The teacher says the sentence slowly and the learners repeat. Then the teacher says the phrase a little faster until the phrase is being said at normal speaking speed.

2. The teacher varies the way of choosing who is to repeat the sentence. The teacher says the sentence and points to the first person in the first row to repeat it. The teacher says it again and points to the second person in the first row. Then the teacher starts pointing at people at random so that the learners cannot predict who will be the next person called on. This variation can also include choosing individuals or choosing the whole class to repeat the sentence. Another variation of this kind is to get the learner who just repeated the sentence to call the name of the next person to repeat the sentence.

3. The teacher can vary the content of the sentence. That is, the teacher can substitute a word for one of the words in a sentence. So instead of only saying "Where is the train station?" the learners might also be called on to repeat "Where is the Post Office?" This is called a Substitution drill.

4. The teacher varies the way the substitution is signaled to the learners, for example, on the board there may be a substitution table like this:

   Where is

   - the station?
   - the post office?
   - your house?
   - the bank?
   - the hospital?

   At first the teacher points to the words "the station" on the board and says "Where is the station?" The learners repeat. The teacher points to the next substitution, "the post office," and says that and the learners repeat. After doing this for a while, the teacher just points to the substitution and does not say it, but the learners have to say the whole sentence. After doing that for a while the teacher does not point but just says the substitution.

5. The teacher may vary the way of choosing the substitution. At first, the teacher chooses the substitutions in the same order as they are written on the board. Then the teacher may choose them in random order so that the learners cannot predict what the next substitution will be.

The Role of Drills

The skill of a teacher in carrying out a drill lies in learning when to vary the activity so that the learners do not become bored by it. Skilled teachers make continual, small variations so that the activity is always challenging, smooth, and interesting. The activity can be taken a step towards a more meaning-focused activity by getting the learners to choose their own words to substitute for words in the model sentence.

The 1970s saw the first steps away from (among other teacher-centered approaches) audiolingualism, a method of teaching that sees the role of the teacher as "central and active . . . [who] provides models, controls direction and pace". In this methodology, teacher-centered drill activities play a large role in the curriculum. With the rise recently of more student-centered approaches – "which are characterized by the involvement of the learner, and the utilization of information about the learner in all aspects of the curriculum" – repetition and substitution drills have come to be considered old-fashioned and (worse still) not useful for language learning.

While acknowledging the contribution that audiolingualism has made, Stern essentially argues against its use: "It's theoretical base was found to be weak. But also in practical terms its hopes had not been fulfilled. Empirical research did not conclusively establish its superiority, and teachers using audiolingual materials . . . complained about the lack of effectiveness of the techniques in the long run and the boredom they engendered among the students" . Moreover, on the role of the teacher in the classroom, Widdowson writes: "It is widely accepted that is undesirable to force learning into conformity with the teacher's preconceived ideas, and it is preferable for the teacher to adapt to the learner rather than the reverse".

The use of drills, however, should be seen as merely one kind of form-focused activity that needs to be balanced with other types of form-focused activities, as well as with meaning-focused and fluency development activities. Drills play a useful part in a language course in helping learners to be formally accurate in their speech and in helping them to quickly learn a useful collection of phrases and sentences that allow them to start using the language as soon as possible. As their proficiency and experience in the language develop, most of these sentences and phrases may be re-analyzed and incorporated into the learners' system of knowledge of the language. Language use based on memorization can be the starting point for more creative use of the language.

Meaning-Focused Speaking

In addition to form-focused speaking, language learners should also be exposed to and given opportunities to practice and use meaning-focused communication, in which they must both produce and listen to meaningful oral communication. An example of a meaning-focused activity for beginning students is Speaking by numbers. Each learner is given a number and a topic. The topics could include family, money, coming to school, a color, future goals, travel, work, and so forth. The learners can think about their topics for a minute or two and then the teacher calls a number. The learner with that number then says two or three sentences about his or her particular topic. The speaker then calls a number and the learner with that number has to ask the speaker a question or two related to the topic just spoken about. When the question is answered, the questioner calls a number and the person with that number asks another question. This continues three or four times and then the speaker calls the number of a new person who will speak about the topic that she or he was given.

This is a meaning-focused speaking activity because both the speaker's and the listeners' attention is on the message being communicated.

Developing the Learner's Knowledge of Language Items

A problem in meaning-focused speaking activities is making sure that the activity is actually developing the learner's knowledge of language items. There are several ways of using speaking to increase the speaker's control of the language items.

1. The meaning-focused speaking activity follows some form-focused instruction. That is, the teacher presents some new vocabulary or grammatical features, gives the learners some practice, and then uses a meaning-focused activity to help the learners use and remember these items.
2. Before the learners speak on a topic or take part in an activity, they work in pairs or groups of three of four

to prepare. This gives the learners the chance to learn new items from each other. Here is an example using a Same or different information gap activity. In this kind of activity the learners work in pairs. Learner A has a set of small numbered pictures. Learner B has a similar set except that while some of B's are exactly the same as A's, some are different. They should sit facing each other so that they cannot see each other's picture(s). Learner A describes the first picture and B listens and then says if her picture is the same or different. If it is the same they both write S next to their picture; if it is different they both write D. Then Learner B describes picture number 2 and they decide if the pictures are the same or different. After they have done five or ten pictures, they can change partners so that Learner A works with a new Learner B. Before the activity begins, all the Learner As can get together in groups and help each other describe their pictures. All the Learner Bs do the same. When they have had enough preparation and practice they form Learner A and B pairs and do the activity.

3. The learners are given topics to talk about. They prepare at home, using dictionaries, reference texts, reading sources, and so forth. Here is an example called Newspaper talks. Each learner has to choose a short and interesting article from an English language newspaper to present to the class. The learner must not read the article aloud to the class but must describe the main points of the article. The class should then ask the presenter questions.

4. Many speaking activities involve some kind of written or picture input in the form of a worksheet. In the Same or different activity this is two sheets of pictures. In a Ranking activity or a Problem Solving activity, the

worksheet contains written data about the situation, what to do, and possible choices. In a "Who Gets the Heart" activity, for example, a group of three or four students must decide from a list of several possible candidates who is to receive the only available heart for transplantation. None of the patients will survive without the new heart. They are a Nobel Prize winner in medical research (a 59 year old male with no family), a homemaker of three (32 year old female), an Olympic athlete (24 year old female, married with no children), an Academy award winning film director (female, 37 years old, two children), and a 45 year old homeless male. The students must rank in order which of these people is most deserving of the heart. Then, each student presents his/her case to the group. Based on these presentations, and the ensuing discussion, the group must choose one candidate for the transplant. Then, each group must present its conclusion to the class as a whole.

The worksheets contain vocabulary and phrases that may be new to the learners and which will be necessary or useful in the speaking activity. For example, in the Ranking activity, the vocabulary in the list of items to rank will need to be used by the learners. Those items which generate the most disagreement over the ranking will likely result in the greatest amount of vocabulary learning. According to Joe, Nation and Newton: "Negotiation of word meaning indicates that an item is noticed and that the learner has a gap in his or her knowledge. Items which [are] negotiated [have] a much greater chance of being learned than items which were not negotiated". If the teacher gives careful thought to the placement of new vocabulary in worksheets for speaking activities, there is a very good chance that the vocabulary will be learned during the speaking activity. If the worksheet uses pictures, some of the pictures or parts of pictures can be given labels that can be used in describing the pictures.

5. Some speaking activities encourage learners to ask each other about the meaning of unfamiliar words or constructions. This seeking and giving of explanations is called negotiation. There are similarities between this type of activity and the Same or Different activity in that each learner in a pair or group has different pieces of information for completing the activity. These kinds of activities are given lots of different names including jigsaw tasks, two-way tasks, information gap, and so forth.

   We have looked at five different ways of making meaning-focused speaking tasks contribute to a learner's knowledge of language items. Language can be learned through production (speaking and writing) as well as through reception (listening and reading), but this learning needs to be planned.

Speaking Fluency

Fluency in speaking is the aim of many language learners. Signs of fluency include a reasonably fast speed of speaking and only a small number of pauses and "ums" and "ers." These signs indicate that the speaker does not have to spend a lot of time searching for the language items needed to express the message.

4/3/2 is a useful technique for developing fluency and includes the features that are needed in fluency development activities. First the learners choose a topic or are given a topic with which they are very familiar. The first time that learners use this technique it may be best if the topic involves recounting something that happened to them. This is because the chronological order of the events will make it easier to recall and repeat because the time sequence provides a clear structure for the talk. The learners work in pairs. Learner A tells a story to Learner B and has a time limit of four minutes to do this. B just listens and does not interrupt or question Learner A. When the four minutes are up, the teacher says, "Change partners"; learner A then moves to a new Learner B. The teacher says "Begin" and Learner A tells exactly the same story to the new partner but this time has only three minutes to tell it. When the three minutes are up, the teacher says "Stop. Change partners." With a new partner, Learner A now has two minutes to tell the story. During the three deliveries of the same story, the B learners do not talk and each listens to three different people. When the A learners have given their talk three times, the B learners can now go through the same sequence, this time as speakers.

Research on this activity shows that the learners' speed of speaking increased during the talks (as measured by the number of words per minute), the hesitations they make decrease (as measured by hesitations per 100 words), and surprisingly their grammatical errors in the repeated parts of the talk decrease and they tend to use several, more complex grammatical constructions in the last of the three talks than they did in the first talk.

The features in 4/3/2 that help the development of fluency are the same features that occur in activities to develop listening fluency.

— The activity involves known vocabulary, grammar, and discourse.

- The learners have a high chance of performing successfully at a higher than normal speed.
- There are repeated opportunities to do the same thing.
- Here are other techniques to develop speaking fluency that involve the same features.

In the Headlines activity, students create newspaper "headlines" that will serve as the basis for the speaking activity. The learners all think of an interesting or exciting thing that has happened to them. Using a felt-tipped pen — so that the writing is easily seen — each learner writes a newspaper headline referring to that event.

The teacher should give some examples to help the learners, such as "Burning Bed Brings Joy" and "Forgotten Shoes Never Return." Half of the learners hold their headlines up for the rest of the class to see. Those not holding up a headline go to hear a story behind the headline that interests them. Each story can be told to no more than two people at a time. When the story is done, the listeners should circulate to a second headline that interests them. The tellers will thus have to repeat their story several times. After there has been plenty of opportunity to tell the stories, the other half of the class hold up their headlines and, in similar fashion, tell their stories.

4/3/2 and Headlines rely on repetition of the same story to develop fluency. This kind of fluency is useful for predictable topics that learners may need to speak about. For example, when meeting other people learners may need to talk about themselves, about their country, about the kind of food they eat, about their travels, about their interests and hobbies, and about their experiences. Speaking fluency also needs to be developed for less predictable topics and the Say it! activity is a useful way of doing this.

In Say it!, learners work in groups of about four people. First they read a Say it! text carefully until they have reached a good understanding of it. They discuss their understanding of the text to make sure everything is fairly clear. Then they do the tasks in the Say it! grid, which is a collection of simple verbal tasks related to the reading. One learner chooses a square for the next learner to perform, for example square B2. The learner does this task while the others observe and, when the student has finished, s/he calls a square, for example, A3, for the next learner. This continues with some learners doing the same task several times and with some tasks being done several times by different learners. Often the tasks are like role plays and require the learners to use the vocabulary that was in the reading text, but to use it in a different way. This helps the development of fluency by providing lots of associations with the vocabulary used in the task, that is the associations from the reading text and its discussion, and the associations from the Say it! role play. Although the Say it! activity does not involve large amounts of repetition, it involves preparation by the learners. That is, the learners prepare for the spoken task by studying the written text. This preparation should increase the fluency with which learners do the spoken task.

Error Correction

Some learners may experience difficulty in pronouncing certain sounds and groups of sounds in another language. Some Chinese and Japanese speakers of English, for example, have trouble with /l/ and /r/. Some learners have trouble with the beginning sounds in the words "three" and "they." Giving too much attention to the correction of pronunciation in the early stages of language learning can make learners worried and reluctant to speak because of fear of making errors.

It is worth thinking about why errors occur, because this can help teachers decide what to do about them. The study of errors and their causes is called error analysis.

For each cause listed below, suggestions for the teacher are given in square brackets.

1. The learner makes an error because the learner has not had sufficient chance to observe the correct form or to develop sufficient knowledge of the language system. [Don't correct the learner but give more models and opportunities to observe.]

2. The learner makes an error because the learner has not observed the form correctly. [Give a little correction by showing the learner the difference between the correct form and the learner's error.]

3. The learner makes an error because of nervousness. [Don't correct. Use less threatening activities – or, if and when appropriate, joke with the person/class/yourself to lighten the mood.]

4. The learner makes an error because the activity is difficult, that is, there are many things the learner has to think about during the activity. This is sometimes called cognitive overload. [Don't correct. Make the activity easier or give several chances to repeat the activity.]

5. The learner makes an error because the activity is confusing. Use of tongue twisters, for instance, for pronunciation can be confusing. [Don't correct. Improve the activity.]

6. The learner makes an error because the learner is using patterns from the first language instead of the patterns from the second language. [Give some correction. If there has been plenty of opportunity to develop knowledge of the second language, then some time should be spent on correction to help the learner break out of making errors that are unlikely to change. Errors which are resistant to change are sometimes called fossilized errors and imaginative correction is often needed to break the fossilization. If there has not been a lot of opportunity to develop knowledge of the second language, correct by telling the learner what to look for when observing people using the second language. This is called consciousness raising. It does not actually teach the correct form but makes the learner more aware of what to look for to learn it.]
7. The learner makes an error because the learner has been copying incorrect models. [Correct the learner and provide better models.]

This range of causes shows that the teacher should not rush into error correction, but should consider whether the error is worth the interruption and, if it is, the teacher should consider possible causes and then think of appropriate ways of dealing with the error.

Pronunciation Correction

The teaching and correcting of pronunciation to learners who are past the age of puberty is often a difficult task. The audiolingualism method argues that native-like pronunciation is one of the most important aspects of language proficiency. However, as Ueno reports: "The research on this issue [whether specific instruction can improve students' pronunciation] is inconclusive. In a recent survey . . . almost half of the recent experiments on this subject show no improvement in students' production of target-language sounds". There is some hope that specific pronunciation instruction may be effective in improving students' perception or overall comprehension of the target-language. Moreover, to use a sports metaphor, a beginning tennis player must "develop and automatize basic muscle skills necessary to perform the new physical tasks. Similarly, a language learner must practice the new motor skills involved in producing the sounds of the target language".

The following are simple suggestions for correcting pronunciation.

1. Say "What?" and see if the learner is capable of self-correction.
2. Give the correct form for the learner to copy. If the learner cannot copy it after two or three attempts, then some explanation and guidance may be needed.
3. Explain how to make the correct form and, if necessary, what is wrong with the error. For example, to make the /th/ sound as in "then," say "Put your tongue between your teeth and make a long sound." A variation on this is to tell the learner to look at what you are doing and say, "Put your tongue like this."

Teaching Listening

Instructors want to produce students who, even if they do not have complete control of the grammar or an extensive lexicon, can fend for themselves in communication situations. In the case of listening, this means producing students who can use listening strategies to maximize their comprehension of aural input, identify relevant and non-relevant information, and tolerate less than word-by-word comprehension.

To accomplish this goal, instructors focus on the process of listening rather than on its product.

- They develop students' awareness of the listening process and listening strategies by asking students to think and talk about how they listen in their native language.
- They allow students to practice the full repertoire of listening strategies by using authentic listening tasks.
- They behave as authentic listeners by responding to student communication as a listener rather than as a teacher.
- When working with listening tasks in class, they show students the strategies that will work best for the listening purpose and the type of text. They explain how and why students should use the strategies.
- They have students practice listening strategies in class and ask them to practice outside of class in their listening assignments. They encourage students to be conscious of what they're doing while they complete listening tape assignments.
- They encourage students to evaluate their comprehension and their strategy use immediately after completing an assignment. They build comprehension checks into in-class and out-of-class listening assignments, and periodically review how and when to use particular strategies.
- They encourage the development of listening skills and the use of listening strategies by using the target language to conduct classroom business: making

announcements, assigning homework, describing the content and format of tests.

– They do not assume that students will transfer strategy use from one task to another. They explicitly mention how a particular strategy can be used in a different type of listening task or with another skill.

By raising students' awareness of listening as a skill that requires active engagement, and by explicitly teaching listening strategies, instructors help their students develop both the ability and the confidence to handle communication situations they may encounter beyond the classroom. In this way they give their students the foundation for communicative competence in the new language.

Teaching listening skills is one of the most difficult tasks for any teacher. This is because successful listening skills are acquired over time and with lots of practice. It's frustrating for students because there are no rules as in grammar teaching. Speaking and writing also have very specific exercises that can lead to improved skills. This is not to say that there are not ways of improving listening skills, however they are difficult to quantify.

One of the largest inhibitors for students is often mental block. While listening, a student suddenly decides that he or she doesn't understand what is being said. At this point, many students just tune out or get caught up in an internal dialogue trying translate a specific word. Some students convince themselves that they are not able to understand well and create problems for themselves. They key to helping students improve their listening skills is to convince them that not understanding is OK. This is more of an attitude adjustment than anything else, and it is easier for some students to accept than others. Another important point the teachers try to teach the students (with differing amounts of success) is that they need to listen as often as possible, but for short periods of time. Many teachers like to use this analogy: Imagine you want to get in shape. You decide to begin jogging. The very first day you go out and jog seven miles. If you are lucky, you might even be able to jog the seven miles. However, chances are good that you will not soon go out jogging again.

Fitness trainers have taught us that we must begin with little steps. Begin jogging short distances and walk some as well, over time you can build up the distance. Using this approach, you'll be much more likely to continue jogging and get fit.

Students need to apply the same approach to listening skills. Encourage them to get a film, or listen to an English radio station, but not to watch an entire film or listen for two hours. Students should often listen, but they should listen for short periods - five to ten minutes. This should happen four or five times a week. Even if they don't understand anything, five to ten minutes is a minor investement. However, for this strategy to work, students must not expect improved understanding too quickly. The brain is capable of amazing things if given time, students must have the patience to wait for results. If a student continues this exercise over two to three months their listening comprehension skills will greatly improve.

Two-Way Communication

In authentic two-way communication, the listener focuses on the speaker's meaning rather than the speaker's language. The focus shifts to language only when meaning is not clear. Note the difference between the teacher as teacher and the teacher as authentic listener in the dialogues in the popup screens.

Listening Strategies

Listening strategies are techniques or activities that contribute directly to the comprehension and recall of listening input. Listening strategies can be classified by how the listener processes the input.

Top-down strategies are listener based; the listener taps into background knowledge of the topic, the situation or context, the type of text, and the language. This background knowledge activates a set of expectations that help the listener to interpret what is heard and anticipate what will come next. Top-down strategies include

- listening for the main idea
- predicting
- drawing inferences
- summarizing

Bottom-up strategies are text based; the listener relies on the language in the message, that is, the combination of sounds, words, and grammar that creates meaning. Bottom-up strategies include

- listening for specific details
- recognizing cognates
- recognizing word-order patterns

Strategic listeners also use *metacognitive strategies* to plan, monitor, and evaluate their listening.

- They plan by deciding which listening strategies will serve best in a particular situation.
- They monitor their comprehension and the effectiveness of the selected strategies.

- They evaluate by determining whether they have achieved their listening comprehension goals and whether the combination of listening strategies selected was an effective one.

Listening for Meaning

To extract meaning from a listening text, students need to follow four basic steps:

- Figure out the purpose for listening. Activate background knowledge of the topic in order to predict or anticipate content and identify appropriate listening strategies.
- Attend to the parts of the listening input that are relevant to the identified purpose and ignore the rest. This selectivity enables students to focus on specific items in the input and reduces the amount of information they have to hold in short-term memory in order to recognize it.
- Select top-down and bottom-up strategies that are appropriate to the listening task and use them flexibly and interactively. Students' comprehension improves and their confidence increases when they use top-down and bottom-up strategies simultaneously to construct meaning.
- Check comprehension while listening and when the listening task is over. Monitoring comprehension helps students detect inconsistencies and comprehension failures, directing them to use alternate strategies.

Developing Listening Activities

As you design listening tasks, keep in mind that complete recall of all the information in an aural text is an unrealistic expectation to which even native speakers are not usually held. Listening exercises that are meant to train should be success-oriented and build up students' confidence in their listening ability.

Each activity should have as its goal the improvement of one or more specific listening skills. A listening activity may have more than one goal or outcome, but be careful not to overburden the attention of beginning or intermediate listeners. Recognizing the goal(s) of listening comprehension in each listening situation will help students select appropriate listening strategies.

- *Identification*: Recognizing or discriminating specific aspects of the message, such as sounds, categories of words, morphological distinctions
- *Orientation*: Determining the major facts about a message, such as topic, text type, setting
- *Main idea comprehension*: Identifying the higher-order ideas
- *Detail comprehension*: Identifying supporting details
- *Replication*: Reproducing the message orally or in writing.

Using Multimedia to Teach Listening

Students can use this outline for both in-class and out-of-class listening/viewing activities. Model and practice the use of the outline at least once in class before you ask students to use it independently.

1. Plan for listening/viewing

- Review the vocabulary list, if you have one
- Review the worksheet, if you have one

- Review any information you have about the content of the tape/video

2. Preview the tape/video

- (tape) Use fast forward to play segments of the tape; (video) view the video without sound
- Identify the kind of program (news, documentary, interview, drama)
- Make a list of predictions about the content
- Decide how to divide the tape/video into sections for intensive listening/viewing

3. Listen/view intensively section by section. For each section:

- Jot down key words you understand
- Answer the worksheet questions pertaining to the section
- If you don't have a worksheet, write a short summary of the section

4. Monitor your comprehension

- Does it fit with the predictions you made?
- Does your summary for each section make sense in relation to the other sections?

5. Evaluate your listening comprehension progress

Assessing Listening Proficiency

You can use post-listening activities to check comprehension, evaluate listening skills and use of listening strategies, and extend the knowledge gained to other contexts. A post-listening activity may relate to a pre-listening activity, such as predicting; may expand on the topic or the language of the listening text; or may transfer what has been learned to reading, speaking, or writing activities.

In order to provide authentic assessment of students' listening proficiency, a post-listening activity must reflect the real-life uses to which students might put information they have gained through listening.

- It must have a purpose other than assessment
- It must require students to demonstrate their level of listening comprehension by completing some task.

To develop authentic assessment activities, consider the type of response that listening to a particular selection would elicit in a non-classroom situation. For example, after listening to a weather report one might decide what to wear the next day; after listening to a set of instructions, one might repeat them to someone else; after watching and listening to a play or video, one might discuss the story line with friends.

Use this response type as a base for selecting appropriate post-listening tasks. You can then develop a checklist or rubric that will allow you to evaluate each student's comprehension of specific parts of the aural text.

10

Teaching Reading and Writing

Teaching Reading

Reading is an activity with a purpose. A person may read in order to gain information or verify existing knowledge, or in order to critique a writer's ideas or writing style. A person may also read for enjoyment, or to enhance knowledge of the language being read. The purpose(s) for reading guide the reader's selection of texts. The purpose for reading also determines the appropriate approach to reading comprehension. A person who needs to know whether she can afford to eat at a particular restaurant needs to comprehend the pricing information provided on the menu, but does not need to recognize the name of every appetizer listed. A person reading poetry for enjoyment needs to recognize the words the poet uses and the ways they are put together, but does not need to identify main idea and supporting details. However, a person using a scientific article to support an opinion needs to know the vocabulary that is used, understand the facts and cause-effect sequences that are presented, and recognize ideas that are presented as hypotheses and givens.

Reading is an interactive process that goes on between the reader and the text, resulting in comprehension. The text presents letters, words, sentences, and paragraphs that encode meaning. The reader uses knowledge, skills, and strategies to determine what that meaning is. Reader knowledge, skills, and strategies include:

- *Linguistic competence*: the ability to recognize the elements of the writing system; knowledge of vocabulary; knowledge of how words are structured into sentences
- *Discourse competence*: knowledge of discourse markers and how they connect parts of the text to one another
- *Sociolinguistic competence*: knowledge about different types of texts and their usual structure and content
- *Strategic competence*: the ability to use top-down strategies as well as knowledge of the language (a bottom-up strategy)

The purpose(s) for reading and the type of text determine the specific knowledge, skills, and strategies that readers need to apply to achieve comprehension. Reading comprehension is thus much more than decoding. Reading comprehension results when the reader knows which skills and strategies are appropriate for the type of text, and understands how to apply them to accomplish the reading purpose.

Instructors want to produce students who, even if they do not have complete control of the grammar or an extensive lexicon, can fend for themselves in communication situations. In the case of reading, this means producing students who can use reading strategies to maximize their comprehension of text, identify relevant and non-relevant information, and tolerate less than word-by-word comprehension. To accomplish this goal, instructors focus on the process of reading rather than on its product.

– They develop students' awareness of the reading process and reading strategies by asking students to think and talk about how they read in their native language.

– They allow students to practice the full repertoire of reading strategies by using authentic reading tasks. They encourage students to read to learn (and have an authentic purpose for reading) by giving students some choice of reading material.

– When working with reading tasks in class, they show students the strategies that will work best for the reading purpose and the type of text. They explain how and why students should use the strategies.

– They have students practice reading strategies in class and ask them to practice outside of class in their reading assignments. They encourage students to be conscious of what they're doing while they complete reading assignments.

– They encourage students to evaluate their comprehension and self-report their use of strategies. They build comprehension checks into in-class and out-of-class reading assignments, and periodically review how and when to use particular strategies.

– They encourage the development of reading skills and the use of reading strategies by using the target language to convey instructions and course-related information in written form: office hours, homework assignments, test content.

– They do not assume that students will transfer strategy use from one task to another. They explicitly mention how a particular strategy can be used in a different type of reading task or with another skill.

By raising students' awareness of reading as a skill that requires active engagement, and by explicitly teaching reading strategies, instructors help their students develop both the ability and the confidence to handle communication situations they may encounter beyond the classroom. In this way they give their students the foundation for communicative competence in the new language.

Instruction in Reading Strategies

Instruction in reading strategies is not an add-on, but rather an integral part of the use of reading activities in the language classroom. Instructors can help their students become effective readers by teaching them how to use strategies before, during, and after reading.

Learning about a Text before Really Reading It: Previewing enables readers to get a sense of what the text is about and how it is organized before reading it closely. This simple strategy includes seeing what you can learn from the headnotes or other introductory material, skimming to get an overview of the content and organization, and identifying the rhetorical situation.

Placing a Text in its Historical, Biographical, and Cultural Contexts: When you read a text, you read it through the lens of your own experience. Your understanding of the words on the page and their significance is informed by what you have come to know and value from living in a particular time and place. But the texts you read were all written in the past, sometimes in a radically different time and place. To read critically, you need to contextualize, to recognize the differences between your contemporary values and attitudes and those represented in the text.

Asking Questions about the Content: As students, you are accustomed to teachers asking you questions about your reading. These questions are designed to help you understand a reading and respond to it more fully, and often this technique works. When you need to understand and use new information though it is most beneficial if you write the questions, as you read the text for the first time. With this strategy, you can write questions any time, but in difficult academic readings, you will understand the material better and remember it longer if you write a question for every paragraph or brief section. Each question should focus on a main idea, not on illustrations or details, and each should be expressed in your own words, not just copied from parts of the paragraph.

Examining your Personal Responses: The reading that you do for this class might challenge your attitudes, your unconsciously held beliefs, or your positions on current issues. As you read a text for the first time, mark an X in the margin at each point where you fell a personal challenge to your attitudes, beliefs, or status. Make a brief note in the margin about what you feel or about what in the text created the challenge.

Outlining and summarizing: Outlining and summarizing are especially helpful strategies for understanding the content and structure of a reading selection. Whereas outlining revels the basic structure of the text, summarizing synopsizes a selection's main argument in brief. Outlining may be part of the annotating process, or it may be done separately (as it is in this class). The key to both outlining and summarizing is being able to distinguish between the main ideas and the supporting ideas and examples. The main ideas form the backbone, the strand that hold the various parts and pieces of the text together. Outlining the main ideas helps you to discover this structure. When you make an outline, don't use the text's exact words. Summarizing begins with outlining, but instead of merely listing the main ideas, a summary recomposes them to form a new text. Whereas outlining depends on a close analysis of each paragraph, summarizing also requires creative synthesis. Putting ideas together again – in your own words and in a condensed form – shows how reading critically can lead to deeper understanding of any text.

Evaluating an Argument: All writers make assertions that want you to accept as true. As a critical reader, you should not accept anything on face value but to recognize every assertion as an argument that must be carefully evaluated. An argument has two essential parts: a claim and support. The claim asserts a conclusion – an idea, an opinion, a judgment, or a point of view – that the writer wants you to accept. The support includes reasons (shared beliefs, assumptions, and values) and evidence (facts, examples, statistics, and authorities) that give readers the basis for accepting the conclusion. When you assess an argument, you are concerned with the process of reasoning as well as its truthfulness (these are not the same thing). At the most basic level, in order for an argument to be acceptable, the support must be appropriate to the claim and the statements must be consistent with one another.

Authentic Approaches to Instruction on Reading

For students to develop communicative competence in reading, classroom and homework reading activities must resemble (or be) real-life reading tasks that involve meaningful communication. They must therefore be authentic in three ways.

1. *The reading material must be authentic:* It must be the kind of material that students will need and want to be able to read when traveling, studying abroad, or using the language in other contexts outside the classroom. When selecting texts for student assignments, remember that the difficulty of a reading text is less a function of the language, and more a function of the conceptual difficulty and the task(s) that students are expected to complete. Simplifying a text by changing the language often removes natural redundancy and makes the organization somewhat difficult for students to predict.
2. *The reading purpose must be authentic:* Students must be reading for reasons that make sense and have relevance to them. "Because the teacher assigned it" is not an authentic reason for reading a text. To identify relevant reading purposes, ask students how they plan to use the language they are learning and what topics they are interested in reading and learning about. Give them opportunities to choose their reading assignments, and encourage them to use the library, the Internet, and foreign language newsstands and bookstores to find other things they would like to read.
3. *The reading approach must be authentic*: Students should read the text in a way that matches the reading purpose, the type of text, and the way people normally read. This means that reading aloud will take place only in situations where it would take place outside the classroom, such as reading for pleasure. The majority of students' reading should be done silently.

Students do not learn to read by reading aloud. A person who reads aloud and comprehends the meaning of the text is coordinating word recognition with comprehension and speaking and pronunciation ability in highly complex ways. Students whose language skills are limited are not able to process at this level, and end up having to drop one or more of the elements. Usually the dropped element is comprehension, and reading aloud becomes word calling: simply pronouncing a series of words without regard for the meaning they carry individually and together. Word calling is not productive for the student who is doing it, and it is boring for other students to listen to.

- There are two ways to use reading aloud productively in the language classroom. Read aloud to your students as they follow along silently. You have the ability to use inflection and tone to help them hear what the text is saying. Following along as you read will help students move from word-by-word reading to reading in phrases and thought units, as they do in their first language.
- Use the "read and look up" technique. With this technique, a student reads a phrase or sentence silently as many times as necessary, then looks up (away from the text) and tells you what the phrase or sentence says. This encourages students to read for ideas, rather than for word recognition.

Developing Reading Skills

Language instructors are often frustrated by the fact that students do not automatically transfer the strategies they use when reading in their native language to reading in a language they are learning. Instead, they seem to think reading means starting at the beginning and going word by word, stopping to look up every unknown vocabulary item, until they reach the end. When they do this, students are relying exclusively on their linguistic knowledge, a bottom-up strategy. One of the most important functions of the language instructor, then, is to help students move past this idea and use top-down strategies as they do in their native language. Effective language instructors show students how they can adjust their reading behavior to deal with a variety of situations, types of input, and reading purposes. They help students develop a set of reading strategies and match appropriate strategies to each reading situation.

Strategies that can help students read more quickly and effectively include :

- *Previewing*: reviewing titles, section headings, and photo captions to get a sense of the structure and content of a reading selection
- *Predicting*: using knowledge of the subject matter to make predictions about content and vocabulary and check comprehension; using knowledge of the text type and purpose to make predictions about discourse structure; using knowledge about the author to make predictions about writing style, vocabulary, and content
- *Skimming and scanning*: using a quick survey of the text to get the main idea, identify text structure, confirm or question predictions
- *Guessing from context*: using prior knowledge of the subject and the ideas in the text as clues to the meanings of unknown words, instead of stopping to look them up
- *Paraphrasing*: stopping at the end of a section to check comprehension by restating the information and ideas in the text

Instructors can help students learn when and how to use reading strategies in several ways.

- By modeling the strategies aloud, talking through the processes of previewing, predicting, skimming and scanning, and paraphrasing. This shows students how the strategies work and how much they can know about a text before they begin to read word by word.
- By allowing time in class for group and individual previewing and predicting activities as preparation for in-class or out-of-class reading. Allocating class time to these activities indicates their importance and value.
- By using cloze exercises to review vocabulary items. This helps students learn to guess meaning from context.
- By encouraging students to talk about what strategies they think will help them approach a reading assignment, and then talking after reading about what strategies they actually used. This helps students develop flexibility in their choice of strategies.

When language learners use reading strategies, they find that they can control the reading experience, and they gain confidence in their ability to read the language.

Reading is an essential part of language instruction at every level because it supports learning in multiple ways.

- Reading to learn the language: Reading material is language input. By giving students a variety of materials to read, instructors provide multiple opportunities for students to absorb vocabulary, grammar, sentence structure, and discourse structure as they occur in authentic contexts. Students thus gain a more complete picture of the ways in which the elements of the language work together to convey meaning.

- Reading for content information: Students' purpose for reading in their native language is often to obtain information about a subject they are studying, and this purpose can be useful in the language learning classroom as well. Reading for content information in the language classroom gives students both authentic reading material and an authentic purpose for reading.
- Reading for cultural knowledge and awareness: Reading everyday materials that are designed for native speakers can give students insight into the lifestyles and worldviews of the people whose language they are studying.

When reading to learn, students need to follow four basic steps:

- Figure out the purpose for reading. Activate background knowledge of the topic in order to predict or anticipate content and identify appropriate reading strategies.
- Attend to the parts of the text that are relevant to the identified purpose and ignore the rest. This selectivity enables students to focus on specific items in the input and reduces the amount of information they have to hold in short-term memory.
- Select strategies that are appropriate to the reading task and use them flexibly and interactively. Students' comprehension improves and their confidence increases when they use top-down and bottom-up skills simultaneously to construct meaning.
- Check comprehension while reading and when the reading task is completed. Monitoring comprehension helps students detect inconsistencies and comprehension failures, helping them learn to use alternate strategies.

Developing Reading Activities

Developing reading activities involves more than identifying a text that is "at the right level," writing a set of comprehension questions for students to answer after reading, handing out the assignment and sending students away to do it. A fully-developed reading activity supports students as readers through prereading, while-reading, and post-reading activities.

As you design reading tasks, keep in mind that complete recall of all the information in a text is an unrealistic expectation even for native speakers. Reading activities that are meant to increase communicative competence should be success oriented and build up students' confidence in their reading ability.

Make sure students understand what the purpose for reading is: to get the main idea, obtain specific information, understand most or all of the message, enjoy a story, or decide whether or not to read more. Recognizing the purpose for reading will help students select appropriate reading strategies.

In addition to the main purpose for reading, an activity can also have one or more instructional purposes, such as practicing or reviewing specific grammatical constructions, introducing new vocabulary, or familiarizing students with the typical structure of a certain type of text.

The factors listed below can help you judge the relative ease or difficulty of a reading text for a particular purpose and a particular group of students.

— How is the information organized? Does the story line, narrative, or instruction conform to familiar expectations? Texts in which the events are presented in natural chronological order, which have an informative title, and which present the information following an obvious organization (main ideas first, details and examples second) are easier to follow.

- How familiar are the students with the topic? Remember that misapplication of background knowledge due to cultural differences can create major comprehension difficulties.
- Does the text contain redundancy? At the lower levels of proficiency, listeners may find short, simple messages easier to process, but students with higher proficiency benefit from the natural redundancy of authentic language.
- Does the text offer visual support to aid in reading comprehension? Visual aids such as photographs, maps, and diagrams help students preview the content of the text, guess the meanings of unknown words, and check comprehension while reading.

Remember that the level of difficulty of a text is not the same as the level of difficulty of a reading task. Students who lack the vocabulary to identify all of the items on a menu can still determine whether the restaurant serves steak and whether they can afford to order one.

The activities you use during pre-reading may serve as preparation in several ways. During pre-reading you may:

- Assess students' background knowledge of the topic and linguistic content of the text
- Give students the background knowledge necessary for comprehension of the text, or activate the existing knowledge that the students possess
- Clarify any cultural information which may be necessary to comprehend the passage

- Make students aware of the type of text they will be reading and the purpose(s) for reading
- Provide opportunities for group or collaborative work and for class discussion activities

Pre-reading activities are most important at lower levels of language proficiency and at earlier stages of reading instruction. As students become more proficient at using reading strategies, you will be able to reduce the amount of guided pre-reading and allow students to do these activities themselves.

Match While-reading Activities

In while-reading activities, students check their comprehension as they read. The purpose for reading determines the appropriate type and level of comprehension.

- When reading for specific information, students need to ask themselves, have I obtained the information I was looking for?
- When reading for pleasure, students need to ask themselves, Do I understand the story line/sequence of ideas well enough to enjoy reading this?
- When reading for thorough understanding (intensive reading), students need to ask themselves, Do I understand each main idea and how the author supports it? Does what I'm reading agree with my predictions, and, if not, how does it differ? To check comprehension in this situation, students may
- Stop at the end of each section to review and check their predictions, restate the main idea and summarize the section

- Use the comprehension questions as guides to the text, stopping to answer them as they read.

Many language textbooks emphasize product (answers to comprehension questions) over process (using reading skills and strategies to understand the text), providing little or no contextual information about the reading selections or their authors, and few if any pre-reading activities. Newer textbooks may provide pre-reading activities and reading strategy guidance, but their one-size-fits-all approach may or may not be appropriate for your students. You can use the guidelines for developing reading activities given here as starting points for evaluating and adapting textbook reading activities. Use existing, or add your own, pre-reading activities and reading strategy practice as appropriate for your students. Don't make students do exercises simply because they are in the book; this destroys motivation.

Another problem with textbook reading selections is that they have been adapted to a predetermined reading level through adjustment of vocabulary, grammar, and sentence length. This makes them more immediately approachable, but it also means that they are less authentic and do not encourage students to apply the reading strategies they will need to use outside of class. When this is the case, use the textbook reading selection as a starting point to introduce a writer or topic, and then give students choices of more challenging authentic texts to read as a followup.

Role of Phonics

A reputable body of research substantiates the positive effects of well-designed phonics instruction and provides guidance about the form that instruction should take. The following research conclusions guided the development of Houghton Mifflin's newly published program, Invitations to Literacy:

- Phonics is an essential part of a comprehensive approach to the teaching of reading.
- Phonics instruction needs to be explicit and direct; incidental and opportunistic approaches to developing phonics are less effective.
- Phonics instruction can and must be meaningful, lively, and engaging; phonics should not be equated with repetitious drill or the mindless completion of worksheets.
- In order for children to gain full use of phonics skills they need guidance in integrating them with other word identification skills and in strategically and fluently applying those skills.
- In order for children to gain full use of phonics skills they need many opportunities to apply them to functional and interesting reading and writing activities.
- While the development of phonics and other word identification skills is essential and necessary for skillful, mature reading, it is not sufficient; skillful mature reading must also build upon language, vocabulary, and concept development as well as a variety of thinking skills.

Based on the available research, Houghton Mifflin incorporated into Invitations to Literacy the following essential components of an effective program for development of word identification skills and reading fluency:

In order to learn to read an alphabetical language like English, children must grasp what is called the alphabetic principle – that printed words are not an arbitrary sequence of letters to be memorized, but that letters represent a limited number of speech sounds that combine to form spoken words. Young children do not intuitively grasp this principle nor do they think of spoken words as having any dimension other than meaning. Phonological awareness refers to children's conscious awareness of the fact that spoken words are composed of identifiable units including syllables, rimes, and sounds (phonemes). It also refers to children's ability to manipulate (segment, blend, substitute) those sound units.

In the Kindergarten level of Invitations to Literacy hildren are taught concepts of rhyme and beginning ounds, the most fundamental phonological awareness kills. They also become proficient in blending and segmenting onsets and rimes. In addition to building phonemic awareness, instruction in onsets and rimes prepares children to read words by analogy. In Grade 1, phonological and phonemic skills are extended and refined. As children encounter words they cannot read, they are taught to use their knowledge of letter sound associations and to blend the phonemes into meaningful, spoken words. Segmenting the sounds of the spoken words and representing them with letters are taught and practiced frequently as children grow in their spelling abilities.

Familiarity with print

There are several dimensions of familiarity with print including:

— *Letter Names/Shapes:* Knowledge of letter names is highly associated with success in beginning reading.

In Invitations to Literacy children learn to recognize letters accurately and quickly. Letter names are, in most cases, good clues to letter sound associations. Being able to form letters quickly is important for writing, which reinforces and extends phonological awareness, knowledge of letter/sound associations, and familiarity with the form of written and spoken words.

– *Concepts of Print:* Children become familiar with concepts of letter, word, sentence, and the relationships of printed and spoken words. They develop the understanding that there is a correspondence between the number of words printed and the number of words read, and they are taught to use this concept to track print.

– *High Frequency Vocabulary:* While phonics skills can be used to identify printed words, many frequently used words are not phonically regular; these words must be recognized accurately and quickly. In Invitations to Literacy children are taught these words and have frequent opportunities to practice them in reading for fluency and in their writing.

– *Systematic, Explicit Phonics:* Phonics instruction in Invitations to Literacy is systematic in that it introduces children to more simple, stable letter/sound relationships (e.g., regular consonants) and then introduces more complex and variable elements (e.g., vowels and vowel pairs). Many common letter patterns are highly regular and common (e.g., -it, -en, -og); they are introduced early. All essential phonic elements are taught.

Phonics instruction is explicit; children are directly and clearly taught about relationships between letters and sounds. They have many opportunities to practice and apply these learnings in a variety of ways, including manipulating letters to build words and applying phonics skills to decodable texts and to writing. Through phonics and spelling instruction children develop the ability to segment and blend phonemes and to sound out words by blending letter sounds from left to right.

– *Spelling:* In Invitations to Literacy spelling and phonics are integrally related. Phonics elements that are taught in a unit of instruction are reinforced in spelling instruction in the same unit. In spelling lessons, children learn to carefully process the letters in words from left to right and to segment and blend the sounds the letters represent.

– *Vocabulary*: Beyond the initial stages of learning to read, there is a very strong relationship between knowledge of word meanings and reading comprehension. Vocabulary instruction and learning to derive word meanings from context begin in kindergarten and continue throughout Invitations to Literacy.

– *Fluent Reading*: Decodable text is essential to provide opportunities for children to practice and apply phonic elements in the context of real reading. Invitations to Literacy includes many decodable books for practice with high frequency words and words that use previously taught phonic elements. In addition to a wide variety of reading materials that are part of the program, Invitations to Literacy provides carefully developed reading lists, frequent suggestions to teachers, and extensive communications with the home to encourage the wide independent reading that leads to fluency.

– *Writing*: Writing offers the opportunity to apply phonics and related spelling knowledge. In shared writing and other writing activities, children learn to think about the sounds in words they want to write and to use phonics skills to represent the sounds. As they proofread their writing, they apply spelling patterns and phonic elements they have been taught.

READING ASSESSMENT

Reading ability is very difficult to assess accurately. In the communicative competence model, a student's reading level is the level at which that student is able to use reading to accomplish communication goals. This means that assessment of reading ability needs to be correlated with purposes for reading. A student's performance when reading aloud is not a reliable indicator of that student's reading ability. A student who is perfectly capable of understanding a given text when reading it silently may stumble when asked to combine comprehension with word recognition and speaking ability in the way that reading aloud requires.

In addition, reading aloud is a task that students will rarely, if ever, need to do outside of the classroom. As a method of assessment, therefore, it is not authentic: It does not test a student's ability to use reading to accomplish a purpose or goal. However, reading aloud can help a teacher assess whether a student is "seeing" word endings and other grammatical features when reading. To use reading aloud for this purpose, adopt the "read and look up" approach: Ask the student to read a sentence silently one or more times, until comfortable with the content, then look up and tell you what it says. This procedure allows the student to process the text, and lets you see the results of that processing and know what elements, if any, the student is missing.

Instructors often use comprehension questions to test whether students have understood what they have read. In order to test comprehension appropriately, these questions need to be coordinated with the purpose for reading. If the purpose is to find specific information, comprehension questions should focus on that information. If the purpose is to understand an opinion and the arguments that support it, comprehension questions should ask about those points.

In everyday reading situations, readers have a purpose for reading before they start. That is, they know what comprehension questions they are going to need to answer before they begin reading. To make reading assessment in the language classroom more like reading outside of the classroom, therefore, allow students to review the comprehension questions before they begin to read the test passage. Finally, when the purpose for reading is enjoyment, comprehension questions are beside the point. As a more authentic form of assessment, have students talk or write about why they found the text enjoyable and interesting (or not).

In order to provide authentic assessment of students' reading proficiency, a post-listening activity must reflect the real-life uses to which students might put information they have gained through reading.

— It must have a purpose other than assessment

— It must require students to demonstrate their level of reading comprehension by completing some task

To develop authentic assessment activities, consider the type of response that reading a particular selection would elicit in a non-classroom situation. For example, after reading a weather report, one might decide what to wear the next day; after reading a set of instructions, one might repeat them to someone else; after reading a short story, one might discuss the story line with friends. Use this response type as a base for selecting appropriate post-reading tasks. You can then develop a checklist or rubric that will allow you to evaluate each student's comprehension of specific parts of the text.

Teaching Writing

Writing is a complex process that allows writers to explore thoughts and ideas, and make them visible and concrete. Writing encourages thinking and learning for it motivates communication and makes thought available for reflection. When thought is written down, ideas can be examined, reconsidered, added to, rearranged, and changed. Writing is most likely to encourage thinking and learning when students view writing as a process. By recognizing that writing is a recursive process, and that every writer uses the process in a different way, students experience less pressure to "get it right the first time" and are more willing to experiment, explore, revise, and edit. Yet, novice writers need to practice "writing" or exercises that involve copying or reproduction of learned material in order to learn the conventions of spelling, punctuation, grammatical agreement, and the like. Furthermore, students need to "write in the language" through engaging in a variety of grammar practice activities of controlled nature. Finally, they need to begin to write within a framework "flexibility measures" that include : transformation exercises, sentence combining, expansion, embellishments, idea frames, and similar activities).

Developmental Writing Stages

Obviously, not all students of the same age or grade level write in the same way; students pass through several developmental writing stages:

Stage 1

Novice Writer (unskilled, unaware, teacher-dependent writer)

- has little, if any, individual style
- has little awareness of writing process
- has undeveloped skills and techniques
- seeks approval from teacher
- is reluctant to revise any writing
- believes good writing comes easily

Stage 2

Transitional Writer (transitional, self-involved, self-delineating writer)

- needs support and coaching in order to develop
- learns from modeled behaviors
- is developing a degree of comfort with the craft
- is anxious to stand alone, yet is uncomfortable with peer collaboration
- is developing an awareness of personal needs, interests, and preoccupations

Stage 3

Willing Writer (peer-involved, willing writer)

- is able to collaborate well with others
- requires external feedback to shape progress
- is able to profit from criticism
- is developing objectivity concerning work
- enjoys practicing craft
- is developing a sensitivity to audience

Stage 4

Independent Writer (independent, autonomous writer)

- makes highly objective self-assessments
- has developed a sophisticated personal style
- has developed a writer's voice
- takes risks and experiments
- is self-motivating and self-aware as a writer
- is a craftsperson

Approaches to Teach Writing

There are several approaches to teaching writing that are presented by as follows:

Controlled-to-Free approach

In the 1950s and early 1960, the audio-lingual method dominated second-language learning This method emphasized speech and writing served to achieve mastery of grammatical and syntactic forms. Hence teachers developed and used techniques to enable student to achieve this mastery. The controlled-to-free approach in is sequential: students are first given sentence exercises, then paragraphs to copy or manipulate grammatically by changing questions to statements, present to past, or plural to singular. They might also change words to clauses or combine sentences. With these controlled compositions, it is relatively easy to for students write and yet avoid errors, which makes error correction easy. Students are allowed to try some free composition after they have reached an intermediate level of proficiency. As such, this approach stress on grammar, syntax, and mechanics. It emphasizes accuracy rather than fluency or originality.

Free-writing approach

This approach stresses writing quantity rather than quality. Teachers who use this approach assign vast amounts of free writing on given topics with only minimal correction. The emphasis in this approach is on content and fluency rather than on accuracy and form. Once ideas are down on the page, grammatical accuracy and organization follow. Thus, teachers may begin their classes by asking students to write freely on any topic without worrying about grammar and spelling for five or ten minutes. The teachers does not correct these pieces of free writing. They simply read them and may comment on the ideas the writer expressed. Alternatively, some students may volunteer to read their own writing aloud to the class. Concern for "audience" and "content" are seen as important in this approach.

Paragraph-pattern approach

Instead of accuracy of grammar or fluency of content, the Paragraph-Pattern-Approach stresses on organization. Students copy paragraphs and imitate model passages. They put scrambled sentences into paragraph order. They identify general and specific statements and choose to invent an appropriate topic sentence or insert or delete sentences. This approach is based on the principle that in different cultures people construct and organize communication with each other in different ways.

Grammar-syntax-organization approach

This approach stresses on simultaneous work on more than one composition feature. Teachers who follow this approach maintain that writing can not be seen as composed of separate skills which are learned sequentially. Therefore, student should be trained to pay attention to organization while they also work on the necessary grammar and syntax. This approach links the purpose of writing to the forms that are needed to convey message.

Communicative approach

This approach stresses the purpose of writing and the audience for it. Student writers are encouraged to behave like writers in real life and ask themselves the crucial questions about purpose and audience. Traditionally, the teacher alone has been the audience for student writing. But some feel that writers do their best when writing is truly a communicative act, with a writer writing for a real reader. As such, the readership may be extended to classmate and pen pals.

Process approach

The teaching of writing has moved away from a concentration on written product to an emphasis on the process of writing. Thus, writers ask themselves:

- How do I write this?
- How do I get started?

In this approach, students are trained to generate ideas for writing, think of the purpose and audience, write multiple drafts in order to present written products that communicate their own ideas. Teachers who use this approach give students time to tray ideas and feedback on the content of what they write in their drafts. As such, writing becomes a process of discovery for the students as they discover new ideas and new language forms to express them. Furthermore, learning to write is seen as a developmental process that helps students to write as professional authors do, choosing their own topics and genres, and writing from their own experiences or observations. A writing process approach requires that teachers give students greater responsibility for, and ownership of, their own learning. Students make decisions about genre and choice of topics, and collaborate as they write. During the writing process, students engage in pre-writing, planning, drafting, and post-writing activities. However, as the writing process is recursive in nature, they do not necessarily engage in these activities in that order.

Process of Writing

Pre-writing

Pre-writing, the first stage in the writing process, begins long before the writer puts thoughts into writing. The experiences, observations, and interactions that students have prior to entering the classroom have an impact upon what they will write and how they will write it. Within the classroom, pre-writing prompts and activities can be integrated into the writing process as scaffolds by teachers to help students generate ideas for their writing and to practice the thinking skills inherent in the activity. To initiate thinking and generate possible writing topics, it is important for students to explore ideas for writing topics using a variety of pre-writing strategies, such as the following:

– Brainstorming
– Constructing thought webs and graphic organizers
– Interviewing a person knowledgeable about the topic
– Engaging in peer or teacher-student discussions and conferences
– Listening to music
– Reading about and researching the topic
– Free writing or timed free writing about the topic
– Viewing media such as pictures, movies, and television
– Listing and categorizing information
– Reflecting upon personal experience
– Examining writing models
– Responding to literature
– Role playing and other drama techniques
– Asking the 5 Ws—who, what, where, when and why.

To explore topics about which to write, the teacher may post suggestions on the bulletin board for student reference. He/she may invite students to add their own pre-writing strategies to ideas such as the following:

Brainstorming about people, places, and feelings: Write down or tell a partner the names of people you could describe, then quickly and briefly describe each one. Name several places you have visited and list descriptive words for each place. List and describe some memorable feelings you have had, and explain the situation in which they occurred.

Talking and listening in pairs or groups: Take turns telling about an interesting person, thing, incident, or object. Encourage the listeners to ask questions and add ideas. Record possible writing topics or ideas as they arise during the discussion.

Looking at art: Study paintings, photographs, drawings, or sculpture in magazines or art books. It may even be useful to take a trip to a local museum or art gallery. Jot down notes and questions about the artwork, the artist and the subject, and any topic ideas that come to mind during the observation. It may help to talk over your information and ideas with a partner or small group. Explain to a partner the stories in the art works.

Listening to music: Listen to music you like best or a variety of new and unfamiliar music. Listen to tape recordings or to the radio, closing your eyes and letting the music paint pictures in your mind. Record these images as you listen, or turn off the music and quickly record your ideas. It may be helpful to tell the story you have imagined to a partner or group.

Role playing: Pretend to be any character, ask peers to act as other characters, and dramatize an event or incident, and what happened as a result of that incident or event.

Observing with all senses: Be aware of all that is happening around you, in the classroom, at home, in restaurants, in malls, and wherever you go. Listen closely to conversations of the people you observe, and try to capture the details of their manners and dress. Observe for issues, problems, or achievements in your community. Jot down ideas and notes as you observe them or as soon as possible after your observations.

Listing ideas and information: List such things as the activities that interest you, the sports you play, the clubs that you belong to, and the community and world issues that you know about from the media.

Reading: Read such things as nonfiction books, novels, magazines, stories, newspapers, and poems. Jot down ideas that occur to you as you read and list questions you might investigate further. Keep track of interesting vocabulary, story plots, and characters.

Newspaper searches: Read the stories and captions that catch your interest. Jot down ideas for writing a newspaper article or ideas that can be developed into other kinds of writing.

Author visits: As the authors share their writing and discuss the craft of writing, students gain further understanding of the writing process and possibly get ideas for their own writing. Pre-writing prompts or activities planned by the teacher can serve as writing scaffolds for inexperienced writers who have difficulty accessing their own feelings, ideas, experiences, and knowledge. Teacher-planned pre-writing activities, such as the samples that follow, give students a place to start and make them become aware of places from which to get ideas in the future. Students who have a place to start with will be more motivated to continue developing their ideas and their own writing voices.

Drafting

After students have generated some ideas, they must decide what they will say about their chosen topic. Students develop an initial plan for the product they will compose.

As they do so, they must consider the purpose, audience, point of view, and format because these elements have implications for both the planning and the drafting of the written product. To develop an initial plan for drafting, students organize the information they have generated during pre-writing by using such structures as outlines, story frames, maps, diagrams, charts, and concept webs. To consider purpose, students write to express ideas, feelings, emotions, and opinions, and they must ask themselves, "What is my purpose for writing this piece?" Some purposes for students' writings are:

1. to express personal feelings or viewpoints
2. to imagine "What if ...?"
3. to narrate
4. to entertain and/or amuse
5. to describe
6. to inform or explain
7. to persuade or convince
8. to request
9. to inquire or question
10. to explore and experiment with ideas and formats
11. to clarify thinking.

To consider audience, students must consider who they are writing for and students must ask themselves, "Who is my intended audience?" Some possible audiences are:

1. *familiar, known audiences*: self, friends, peers, family, teachers
2. *extended, known audiences*: community, student body, local media

3. *extended, unknown audiences*: wider range of media and other publications

To consider point of view, students must determine from which point of view their ideas or information will be expressed, so they need to ask themselves, "Who is telling this story/describing the events?" Some points of view for students' consideration are:

1. physical point of view: where is the narrator in relation to the action?

2. objective and subjective point of view: what emotional involvement does the narrator have in relation to the situation?

3. personal point of view: who is the narrator of the story?

To decide what information will be gathered and how it will most effectively be gathered, students who decide that they need to conduct interviews or go on field trips to gather information will need to brainstorm and construct a list of questions. Students who require library research will need to decide the types of resources and references to consult. To consider format, students will use audience and purpose to determine format and genre. They will have the opportunity to write in a variety of narrative, descriptive, expository, and poetic formats.

At this point in the process, the emphasis is on content and meaning rather than on mechanics and conventions. This is the time for writers to get down their ideas and thoughts, composing rough drafts based upon pre-writing and planning activities and considerations. As they compose, writers begin to determine what to include and exclude, and make initial decisions about how these ideas will be organized. During the drafting stage of the writing process, meaning begins to evolve.

- To produce a first, rough draft, students record their ideas rapidly in order to capture the essence of what they have to say. They do not have to make any attempt to revise or edit at this point. They focus on talking to the reader and begin to develop a personal style as their voices emerge.
- To write subsequent drafts, students often accomplish their work by crossing out, adding, and rearranging ideas directly on the page. The students' redrafting does not necessarily require an entire rewrite at this time.
- To reflect upon their own writing, students can conference with self, peers and the teacher. Through conferencing, students can get constructive feedback and support that may help them to shape their writings.

Post-writing

When students have an authentic audience and purpose, they want to rework their written drafts, polishing them for presentation or publication. Going public means taking a huge risk; the student's self-esteem is on the line, so the decision about how and with whom to share their writing must be up to the student writer. Teachers may encourage students to share certain pieces or determine the number of pieces that students are required to share or publish within a set time period, but ultimately the decision about which pieces to share, and with whom, should be left up to the writer. To prepare a final, polished draft, students may write in legible handwriting or use a word-processing program to prepare a polished written work. Then their writings go to public through sharing, publishing and using a portfolio.

Sharing: Students may share their written work. Sharing is a useful post- writing activity since it provides students with an immediate audience. Some examples of sharing students' writings include

1. The author's chair, which provides opportunity for students to share their writing aloud with the whole class;
2. Sharing in small groups or with a partner; and
3. Using bulletin board space assigned to a specific genre or to a class of students.

At times, students should be provided with opportunities to decide if they wish to share their written work, and whether they will share in pairs, in small groups, or with the whole class.

Publishing: Students may choose to publish their writing. Some examples of publishing formats include:

- Class booklets
- School or local newspapers
- Yearbook
- Writing contests
- Magazines

Using a portfolio: To decide if the written work will be placed in the student's assessment portfolio, teachers can negotiate with students to generate guidelines about the number and variety of pieces that they are required to place in their portfolio for assessment and evaluation purposes. Contracts may be useful to address individual student needs and abilities. Students should be involved in making choices about which of their written pieces will become part of their portfolios.

Bibliography

Angeles-Bautista, Fenny delos (ed.), *The multigrade teacher's handbook*, BEE/DECS/UNICEF: Philippines, 1994.

Bacharach N., Hasslen R. C., Anderson J., *Learning together: A manual for multiage grouping*, Corwin Press Inc, Thousand Oaks, California, 1995.

Basic Primary Education Project, *Multigrade teacher training manual (for teachers)*, Primary Teacher Training Unit, Sanothimi, Nepal, 2000.

Collingwood, I., "Multiclass teaching in primary schools: a handbook for teachers in the Pacific", *UNESCO Office for the Pacific States: Apia, Western Samoa*, 1991.

Gritzman, Nicki, "Teaching in the Multigrade Classroom", *A Pack of Materials to Support Teachers in Multigrade Classrooms in Stann Creek District, Belize*. Belize Teacher's Training College, Belize, 1998.

Kich Pham Vu et al, *Teacher Training Modules on methods and techniques of multigrade teaching and learning*, Module 4, module 5, module 6, UNICEF: Hanoi, 1995.

Miller, Bruce A., "The multigrade classroom: a resource handbook for small rural schools Regional Educational Laboratory: Oregon", USA, 1989.

Son, V., Pridmore P., Nga, B.. My D., and Kick P., "Renovating the teaching of health in multigrade primary schools: A teacher's guide to health in natural and social sciences

(Grades 1,2,3) and Science (grade 5)", British Council / National Institute of Educational Sciences: Hanoi, Vietnam. full text, 2002.

Thomas, Christopher; Shaw, Christopher, "Issues in the development of multigrade schools", *World Bank Technical Paper* 172: Washington, 1992.

UNESCO/APEID, "Multiple class teaching in primary schools: a methodological guide", *UNESCO Principal Regional Office for Asia and the Pacific: Bangkok,* 1988.

Index

